MODERN WEAPONS CACHING

MODERN WEAPONS CACHING

A Down-to-Earth Approach to Beating the Government Gun Grab

RAGNAR BENSON

Paladin Press • Boulder Colorado

Also by Ragnar Benson:

Acquiring New ID
Do-It-Yourself Medicine
Eating Cheap
Guerrilla Gunsmithing
Hard-Core Poaching
Live Off the Land in the City and Country
Mantrapping
Modern Survival Retreat
Most Dangerous Game
Ragnar's Action Encyclopedia, Vol. 1
Ragnar's Action Encyclopedia, Vol. 2
Ragnar's Guide to Interviews, Investigations, and Interrogations
Ragnar's Guide to the Underground Economy
Ragnar's Tall Tales
Ragnar's Ten Best Traps
Ragnar's Urban Survival
Starting a New Life in Rural America
Survival Nurse
Survival Poaching
The Survival Retreat
Survivalist's Medicine Chest
Switchblade: The Ace of Blades, Revised and Updated (with Michael Janich)

Modern Weapons Caching:
A Down-to-Earth Approach to Beating the Government Gun Grab
by Ragnar Benson

ISBN 13: 978-0-87364-583-6
Printed in the United States of America

Published by Paladin Press, a division of
Paladin Enterprises, Inc.,
P.O. Box 1307
Boulder, Colorado 80306 USA
+1.303.443.7250

Direct inquiries and/or orders to the above address.

Contents

Introduction

Weapons caching has been an important strategy in at least two of the major wars fought in the past fifty years.

Initially, it may seem strange to view weapons caching as having a significant impact on World War II, but in the case of occupied France from 1940 to 1944, the willingness and ability of the French Resistance to take delivery of weapons, move them around the country, and then safely store them against the day of need contributed in part to the defeat of the Nazis. Although the Resistance efforts were considered by many to be relatively puny (they used only three thousand pounds of C-4 for their entire operation, less than one goodsized bomb from a B-24 Liberator), they were more effective at sabotaging the Nazi war effort by stopping the production and flow of munitions than the entire bomber command, and inadvertent civilian casualties from Resistance activities were very light.

The Resistance organized very quickly after the occupation of France in June 1940. Because the French, like the English, had little history of private firearm ownership, there were few weapons on hand with which to commence action. (Historical records show that some farmers had shotguns, but virtually none owned pistols or rifles legally.) The first British agent into Paris radioed back that they had "but two revolvers and two rifles." This appraisal may not have been entirely accurate, but it was the one accepted by the English.

Initially, only the French Communists were organized enough to carry out a credible program of opposition to the Germans. (Some historians downplay their role, but it was the Communists against the Fascists, and the United States supported the Communists.)

Some thirty years later, the United States lost in Vietnam, in part because of the elaborate, careful, weapons caches set up in patient, thorough, oriental fashion by the Vietnamese. Like the Resistance in World War II, the able, careful Vietcong made great use of weapons caches to defeat an opponent that thought itself smarter, better organized, and more technologically advanced.

Correlations between the Vietcong, who were Stalinist Communists, and members of the French Resistance, who were more Trotsky-like, are perhaps coincidental; at the very least the link is ironic. Nevertheless, like the French before them, burying weapons was, for the Vietnamese, a key tactical strategy. Each time they suffered reversal, their weapons went safely underground, beneath flooded rice paddies, or into the swamps.

Weapons caching technologies have changed dramatically since World War II. Methods of resealing containers and evacuating moisture have advanced to the point that technological problems are no longer a consideration. Caching difficulties with which the French Resistance labored mightily can be handled today without much thought as to what we would do without inexpensive plastic pipe, fittings, moisture-absorbing chemicals, and modern greases.

The Resistance had to work with heavy, clumsy, shiny aluminum tubing that cracked, corroded, leaked, and bent out of shape, creating almost insurmountable opening and reclosing problems. Modern plastic pipe and fittings found in plumbing supply shops alleviate these problems to a large extent. Like its aluminum predecessor, most plastic pipe is so tough it can be dropped out of a plane.

Because technologies related to locating a cache have also made quantum leaps, the person whose strategy includes weapons caching must now spend more time and energy deciding where to place a cache. This is in contrast to World War II, when the Resistance had to give as much thought to how the cache would be built as to where it would be placed.

Based upon the great emphasis some law enforcement people place on thoroughly searching a suspect's home, yard, and grounds with sensitive electronic devices, official searchers and seekers appear to have identified weapons caching as a particularly threatening activity. These officials seem to have learned the lessons of history better than average citizens suspect.

Americans in Vietnam knew the Vietcong were getting weapons from irregular caches, and they learned that they needed to locate these caches whenever possible. Today many Americans realize the United States is in a race against firearms confiscation in which the lessons of the past will play a significant role. This book is dedicated to those who wish to look to the future with both mistrust and a will to prevail.

CHAPTER ONE

The French Resistance

We don't know Madeleine's entire name. When she filed her story for the record in 1966, she still wished to maintain a great deal of anonymity. Now, twenty-five years after the writing, and forty-seven years after her incident, it is impossible to pinpoint exact dates or even last names.

In 1943, when she was first active in the French Resistance, she was but eighteen years old. In all likelihood, Madeleine was a Communist, but to what extent can a girl of eighteen be philosophically and religiously committed to communism? As events proved, she was very committed to a liberated France.

Her code name was Renee. She was with the area Resistance leader when he was shot dead by the Germans. Michel (his code name) made the mistake of bolting like a scared fox from the foot of a bridge they were about to blow up. He ran straight across the bridge, giving the guards a clear field of fire. Renee escaped unharmed through a thick, tangled hedge. The explosives they had intended to use came from a mine in northern France, where they were cached by another group whom Renee did not know. She was the only remaining member of her little central Paris band who knew the locations of the various weapons caches, as well as the identity of their parallel cells.

At her age and station in life she did not (even passively) seek out a position of leadership, but she knew that with most of the men still in prisoner of war camps, it was up to women like her to carry on the work of the Resistance. Her life was made no less difficult by an almost immediate directive relayed by message to every Resistance member in the Paris regional group: "You are ordered to kill one German."

Renee picked two stout table knives from amongst the flatware in her apartment. (Perhaps one could do the job, but she wanted to be certain.) She hoped the dark, tattered clothes she wore made her look much older and less conspicuous. Slowly, stooped and shuffling, she picked her way down the street. Two blocks away, Renee slipped into a short, seldom-used blind alley off of one of Paris' lesser streets. The few windows were either boarded or so grimed over with dirt that little light could pass through.

Acting quickly now, Renee squatted down, using her full skirt to obscure the view back to the street. Pulling the knives from her pocket, she began cutting the greasy dirt and grime from around the twenty-second tile, counting from a small smudge on the dirty brown stucco wall. After a moment or two, she was able to raise the tile with the knife blade. Beneath it, under an inch or two of clay, was a small, rectangular tin box.

The box contained one fully loaded 8mm Modele d'Ordonnage 1892 revolver. It was one of two weapons the group possessed. This particular pistol had been in storage for many months now. Renee noticed that the wooden grips had started to crumble as a result of the street moisture settling in a spot where handling had wiped the Cosmoline away. She did not know who originally cached the weapons, but she supposed they were hidden prior to the occupation.

Unbeknownst to Renee, the revolver was, because of its limited power and small ammunition capacity, considered substandard by French authorities. It had found its way into Resistance hands only because other potential users had no use for it.

After spending the night practicing a dry-fire routine with the weapon, Renee climbed on her bicycle and pedaled to Pont de Solferino, a bridge over the Seine, for her appointment with the Gestapo chief. (French sport fishermen had reported that a Gestapo major customarily strolled the Seine every Sunday morning, usually stopping at Pont de Solferino to watch them catch fish.)

Predictably, the major was leaning on the rock walls smoking while he surveyed the anglers. He straightened a bit when he heard her shoes clacking on the cobblestones behind. As he turned, she fired point-blank into his face. The tough old Prussian stood like a stone statue rather than falling. She fired again into his chest. Now he was down. There were no sounds of alarm. The two, as far as she could tell, were alone. Even the fishermen paid little heed.

Renee fought the instinct to run immediately; the Resistance desperately needed additional arms. It didn't take long to strip the major's Luger from its holster and place it in her handbag with the revolver.

On a desperate run now, she jumped on her bicycle and pedaled off furiously down the quay. The only sound was of an automobile coming up the street behind her.

Quickly and efficiently, the car sideswiped the bike, crumpling it and sending the girl skidding along the street. Kneeling on the pavement, she tried to retrieve one of the spilled weapons and fire it into her assailant.

Before she could shoot, a French police officer twisted her arms behind her back and secured them with handcuffs. Renee had suffered the intense bad luck of running into an officer out for a quiet drive with his mistress.

Automobile traffic in occupied Paris was extremely light, and Renee was somewhat relieved to arrive at the police prefecture in three minutes. (The nervous mistress had held her at gunpoint, a situation Renee rightly perceived to be very dangerous.)

She was turned over to a squad of Gestapo-trained French collaborators. (After the war, most of these people were tried and executed for their activities, but at the time they played the role of expert interrogators for the Germans.) However, due to the spirit and strength of the Resistance and the rumored imminent landing of the Allies, they chose not to mistreat her physically. By one elaborate subterfuge after another they tried to trick, cajole, or threaten the name of her section chief out of her. Little did her French tormenters know that this young girl was, in fact, the section leader.

"I was outraged by German atrocities in France," she repeated over and over, "so I decided to kill a German. I saw the officer and I killed him." Later, she shortened her account to a simple, "I don't know anything."

After her captors tired of this game, they turned her over to the Germans. She was marched into a bare room and ordered to strip naked. The shame of standing naked for the first time before men was worse than that of taking a human life. Slowly and methodically, the men pulled her hair out, burned her feet, and submerged her head in a tub of ice water. Through it all, she bled and festered, but she never said more than "I don't know anything."

Their last desperate attempt involved bringing in a recently captured sixteen-year-old boy whom Renee knew was a collaborator in her own section. They had never met, however, so there was no danger she would be recognized. Their meeting was one of those coincidences that happen in times of war. As promised, her professional Gestapo interrogators broke every bone in the boy's hands, feet, arms, and legs while she was forced to watch. Yet Renee held to her story until finally and mercifully the lad was dispatched with a shot to the head. That afternoon the Gestapo gave up and sent her to Fresines Prison under sentence of death.

Renee was liberated when the Allies landed and the Germans retreated with more urgent matters on their minds.

In spite of brutal repressions of this sort, the Resistance continued to grow. Although initially slow getting out of the blocks, the Free French and the Allies did eventually open the weapons supply pipeline, getting considerable tonnage of supplies through to the Resistance.

During all of 1941, the Royal Air Force (RAF) dropped a miserably small number of two-hundred pound aluminum cylinders to the Resistance in France—9, to be exact. In 1942, when they finally understood the program, they dropped 201 containers.

From January 1943 until liberation, heaven's gates were opened as literally thousands of containers full of explosive manna rained down from the many Stirlings, Wellingtons, Halifaxes, and Dakotas sent over occupied France. Even the U.S. Army Air Force helped with this supply mission, after initially claiming that the risks were not worth the potential gain.

By late 1943, the Resistance was collectively assassinating an average of one German soldier per day in Paris alone. They were derailing trains on a regular basis, destroying factories, and disrupting power supplies. As a result of their efforts, telephone service was virtually non-

Cache tubes tilled with weapons are loaded into airplanes to be dropped to Resistance fighters who will either store the arms or press them into immediate service. (Photo courtesy of Imperial War Museum, London, England.)

existent. German field units were forced to use radios, which could be monitored in the U.K.

Various load configurations were used, but the standard two-hundred-pound cache cylinder usually contained the following:

- 6 Bren guns, 78 extra magazines, and 1,000 rounds per gun
- 36 Enfield rifles with 150 rounds per gun
- 27 Sten guns, 100 extra magazines, 300 rounds per gun, and 16 loaders
- 5 Enfield pistols with 50 extra rounds per gun

Toward the end of the war the Parisians often met en masse to train, parade, and plan. A number of the weapons they display were captured from the enemy. (Photo courtesy of Imperial War Museum, London, England.)

40 standard hand grenades
12 heavy hand grenades
18 pounds of plastique with caps and fuzes
156 field dressings
6,600 rounds of 9mm ammo
3,168 rounds of .303 ammo

Reports from the pick-up agents in the field claimed that no matter how they tried, they were never able to repack everything into the tubes. The British packers utilized every square inch of space. Often the recipients made the mistake of immediately opening the tubes to

Rifles, Sten guns, Bren guns, and mortars are packed into cache tubes for delivery to the French Resistance. (Photo courtesy of Imperial War Museum, London, England.)

check for damage, forcing them to carry parts of the cache by hand because they would not all fit back in the tube.

Most drops were made by air. Some supplies were sent in by sea, but because German activities were especially intense within twenty-five miles of the coast, these actions were limited. British commandos placed several caches of munitions in shallow, offshore locations, marking them with buoys of the type commonly used for lobster pots. One cache was found by fishermen who turned it in to the Germans for a generous cash reward. Another was found by members of the Resistance, who immediately made good use of it. A third cache of supplies, not recovered until a year after its deposition, was ruined. Apparently, the only agent who knew of its existence and location was inadvertently parachuted onto the roof of Gestapo headquarters. He survived but was not released in time to get to the weapons before the corrosive saltwater did. Limited caching technology of that era required that people give fully as much thought to where a cache was placed as to how it might be constructed.

Resistance cache builders ranged from cavalier to cautious with regard to their activities. In all cases, it was essential that the weapons be distributed and stored quickly. The Resistance estimated that, as a general rule, 10 percent of their deliveries was lost to the enemy, 10 percent was just plain lost, 20 percent was used immediately, and 60 percent was stored for future need. When the Allies landed at Normandy, these caches were bulging with enough arms and munitions to set up an internally generated Free French army. In this case, long-term caching was a major strategy that the French executed purposefully and successfully.

Now and again, reports filter out of modern France of accidental findings of an ancient Resistance arms cache uncovered in an old cellar excavation or a road cut. In general, however, most munitions landed and cached were ultimately recovered and used.

Resistance officers almost universally believed that farmers and rural people would do the best job of hiding weapons. Therefore, as a rule, they usually attempted to place caches on farms, in barns, and in other rural settings. Most French citizens supported the Resistance in concept if not out in the field. It was unlikely that German authorities would be notified of suspicious movements

At times, the cachers took incredible risks. Weapons were stored in wooden military crates inside barns, milking parlors, and horse stalls like so many bales of hay. Many had little more than a light straw covering or a cloth tarp to keep them from the eyes of casual observers. Under such circumstances, Resistance leaders argued that the weapons were being issued as quickly as possible and that the open storage was only very temporary. Once the end users got hold of them, it became their duty to be sure their weapon was not discovered.

Nevertheless, keeping guns, ammo, and explosives out in almost plain view displayed an incredible amount of bravado, especially given the severe penalties one could expect for being caught with war materiel. Officially, it was a matter of policy for the Resistance that one never carried a weapon or explosive unless engaging in an actual preplanned operation. Those who violated the rule and were caught by the Gestapo quickly found themselves in death camps in eastern Germany and Poland. Rules regarding proper caching were, in that manner, strictly enforced.

Problems became especially severe in cities, where the number of Resistance members able to use firearms dwindled rapidly as a result of death and internment. Practice and training with live ammunition for replacement members was impossible, since the Germans were waging a fairly successful war of attrition.

Captured agents often revealed the location of their caches when subjected to torture. On October 14, 1941, a farmer named DuBove was raided by the Gestapo near the village of Lestiac (fifteen miles from Bordeaux} because a member gave in to torture. A newly arrived agent from England named Charles Hayes was among those at the farm when it was hit by the Gestapo in the wee hours of the morning. Fighting went on for more than three hours as the agent, the farmer, and the farmer's son ran from building to building in an attempt to hold off their attackers.

Here, two women, one armed with an Erma machine pistol, supervise a "free drop," done without a parachute to minimize exposure to the enemy. Initially, the Resistance was run almost entirely by women. (Photo courtesy of Imperial War Museum, London, England.)

The stone house and bam afforded fairly good protection, but eventually everyone, including several female resisters, were too wounded to go on. The men were captured alive and held for a time before being executed at Gross Rosen Prison.

Women were often executed when the Germans were reasonably sure they were involved in the movement of weapons and/or in the Resistance. The following account of four female agents is typical. Vera Leigh, Diana Rowden, Andrea Borrel, and Sonia Olschanesky were arrested for Resistance activities, including the transport of weapons and explosives. They were taken by train to a concentration camp at Natsweler in Alsace. There, a Resistance officer recognized them and made an attempt to talk to them, but the women were immediately whisked away to individual cells, where they were held until late that night.

About 11:00 P.M., they were marched to the crematorium, given a lethal injection, and disposed of in the ovens.

While lax caching methods stand out because of their stupidity, they were the exception rather than the rule. Mistakes, when they occurred, were so costly that few operated under the illusion that they were dealing in a small-time game of chance. Most drops and subsequent caches were very well organized. A classic rendezvous occurred in the fall of 1943. A large number of Resistance members organized a full-blown funeral procession. Using clandestine wireless transmitters, they arranged for a drop near a rural cemetery. The operation took place at daybreak. Scores of mourners dressed in tall hats, black scarves, and gloves carried numerous concealed Sten guns. In spite of wartime rationing, they were able to arrange a motorized hearse with enough fuel for the operation. There were also many horse-drawn conveyances to help move the numerous aluminum cylinders from the landing zone to their cache site.

The weapons were placed in waiting open graves, in a few of the mausoleums, and otherwise scattered around the cemetery. Others were dispatched off with Sten-toting mourners to the various farms and chateaus in the region. For a time, several cases of ammo and C-4 explosive rode along under little more than a covering of flowers. Even though they crossed several police checkpoints, no one questioned the mourners or searched the vehicles. By nightfall, several dozen containers of arms were scattered about the region, ready for deployment.

CHAPTER TWO

Resistance Caching Strategy

Early in their existence, working members of the Resistance discovered that the best weapons cachers were farmers and ex-smugglers, not necessarily in that order. The detection technology of the times was such that it was very difficult for the enemy to locate a well-placed, well-hidden cache.

However, the Nazis sometimes displayed some rudimentary cleverness as they went about their business. In an account told by an English officer (who saw no correlation between free and unencumbered ownership of firearms and effective general resistance to tyranny), a retired French colonel had about twenty hunting rifles in his personal collection stored in a chateau outside of town. All were duly registered at local police headquarters as required by law. Had the Gestapo waited until he started distributing the rifles, they might have made some real trouble for the old war-horse and located several members of the local Resistance in the process. However, a sharp-eyed German sergeant noticed the list and drove immediately out to the farm to confiscate the weapons.

As the Brit tells the tale, the German experienced some difficulty gaining entrance into the colonel's gun room. By the time he did, a fourteen-year-old grandson had pulled all of the bolts from the weapons and thrown them in the lake. (It was lost on the English soldier that the Germans already had plenty of weapons and were not confiscating the rifles for their own use, but to keep them from the French. Therefore, in spite of the outcome, the German purpose was served as a result of the sergeant's drive to the country.)

The Englishman's account concludes with the philosophical deduction that while men are indeed killed as easily as deer with hunting rifles, the English government could not have resupplied the rifle owners with nonstandard ammunition for their weapons even if the bolts had not been thrown in the lake, so neither side gained an advantage as a result of the private ownership of weapons.

In fact, private ownership of weapons was not, insofar as one can determine from contemporary sources, much of a factor in the conduct of the Resistance. Apparently a very few illegal, unregistered pistols were held by the Communists in their various city cells, but they were not of much impact. At the outset of hostilities, all of these went immediately into individual caches. They came out piecemeal for specific purposes or were, as was generally true, augmented by English supply drops. The few shotguns farmers may have owned were too few and ineffective to be much of a military factor.

One would think that with millions of men of the French army under arms before its general collapse, along with the debacle at Dunkirk, that hundreds of thousands of unregistered, untagged weapons would have been floating around France. Apparently, this was not the case. One account does relate that an obscure French corporal wished to distribute military supplies to the general population immediately after Dunkirk but was thwarted in his efforts by a small-town mayor. (Perhaps, as often happens today, his honor wanted mainly to avoid problems and keep the city running smoothly, even if under a dictatorship.)

British Sten guns along with extra magazines are packed into cache tubes for delivery to the Resistance. (Photo courtesy of Imperial War Museum, London, England.)

The majority of weapons utilized by the Resistance came from England and were shipped covered with molten Cosmoline and wrapped in heavy paper. Ammo was sent in hermetically sealed cases. After some trial and error, explosives were delivered in sealed aluminum cans or dipped in a waterproof coating and wrapped in paper. (C-4 is very stable, even without a package to protect it.)

On the other hand, storage technology was so primitive that the Resistance spent a great deal of time finding locations where storage was feasible without deterioration of the weapons, ammunition, and explosives. Resistance cachers found it was best and easiest if they removed the portion of supplies they needed for

Small arms, ammunition, and clothing are packed into cache tubes, which are then packed three each into drop tubes. A master sergeant records what goes where. (Photo courtesy of Imperial War Museum, London, England.)

immediate action from the aluminum cylinders and resealed the remainder intact for burial. Supplies sent to them were packed so meticulously that they found repacking was only possible if at least 20 percent of the goods was removed.

Resistance members used petroleum-based sealant to reseal the aluminum tubes before they went into the ground. This method was only modestly successful. Brand new military supplies shipped in their sturdy original wrapping or coating lasted reasonably well in short-term caches. (Short-term for the Resistance was from one to three months.) Underwater caches were tried off the coast of Brittany with only limited success. At least one container leaked, ruining all of the contents very quickly. After the war, the Allies estimated that only a few tons of materiel came in over the beaches (as compared to thousands of tons in Vietnam).

Personal Caches

Really clever caching schemes were developed when individual Resistance members took single weapons to their homes or places of work. These locations were characterized by false ceilings, special compartments between walls, compartments between floor joists in roof alcoves, and other such hiding places.

As a general rule, finding a good place for one's weapons, a few magazines, or some ammunition was not a significant problem. However, early in the war, one particular characteristic of C-4 caused almost insurmountable problems.

The material gave off a particularly strong odor of almonds. It was a distinctive, almost oily smell that permeated any structure in which the explosive was stored, including barns. Later in the war, when manufacturing techniques were improved, the blocks were coated with paraffin and put into small, more airtight containers. Until then, anyone entering a cache house could and would inevitably detect the presence of explosives.

Unless the arms were immediately deployed to the end user, they were cached—without unwrapping or degreasing—in their newly issued condition, and the ammunition was almost always cached separately. (Separate storage made sense when the weapons were so encrusted with Cosmoline as to be unusable.)

Caches of weapons were maintained in numerous locations throughout the region. The first question asked of suspects by the Gestapo was always, "Where are your weapons hidden?" Resistance members were always careful to know only one or two cache locations. As a rule, one of these was their own personal cache, consisting of a single weapon and some ammunition. In a case of absolute necessity, that cache could be revealed without jeopardizing the supplies of the entire region. (Some Resisters undoubtedly went to the ovens knowing exactly where a cache or two of weapons were hidden, which may account for the surprise discoveries unearthed from time to time today.)

Regional Caches

Larger, regional caches were almost always made in the countryside. Weapons were placed underground at measured distances from a fence or tree in worked ground. Suspicious digging was easier to camouflage in a plowed field. At times, caches were made in ponds, cesspools, and septic tanks; at the bottom of rain barrels; under barn floors; in horse stalls; under haystacks; and wherever else clever farmers could devise to keep the weapons safe from the Gestapo's steely eyes. Later, the survivors claimed that virtually every French farmer who had a mean stallion buried cases of supplies in the horse's stall. German soldiers knew about mean stallions and were content to peek through the panels of the stall as they passed by.

All animal pens were considered good places in which to place caches. A rich, luxurious coating of chicken manure, for instance, provided excellent camouflage for cases containing Piat mortars. Reports were circulated that rabbit pens and goat mangers were often supported on full ammo cans. Pistols and submachine guns were placed in granaries, wood boxes, outhouses, butter churns, stored farm machinery, manure heaps, or just hung in bags from barn lofts.

Farmers also cached weapons in hollow trees, in root cellars, under garage floors, in hedge rows, in chimneys, in hollow areas in stone walls, under foundations, and underground right in the middle of a road. Cylinders full of weapons were often transported in honey wagons, manure spreaders, loads of firewood, bags of grain, and under false floors or straw placed in wagons used to transport livestock.

In rural areas there were endless opportunities for the clever and alert. Some caches were found but, as a general rule, they were successfully obscured and camouflaged, in spite of the fact that the Germans often brought in sophisticated electronic mine-locating devices in their attempts to find Resistance caches.

In the city it was an entirely different matter. Because of pipes, reinforcing rods, nails, bolts, and other construction materials, the Gestapo's attempts to employ metal detection equipment were generally foiled. On the other hand, city dwellers usually had far less territory over which to spread an arms cache, especially if several cylinders were involved. Places where a cache might be set up were usually fairly obvious to those who had already uncovered one or two or had worked for the team setting them up.

Because most of the Communist cells were in the cities, immediate movement of weapons, both into caches and into the end user's hands in the city, was especially urgent. Agents trained in England were specifically instructed to be mindful of the need for a good, remote secure drop site, the requirement to move the newly arrived weapons to safe cache sites, and the ability to move the individual items into the cities as needed. Caching near a bakery or dairy with regular home-delivery routes was especially common.

Some city resisters built compartments in wine and beer barrels, sewer systems, and chimneys, or constructed false backs in clothes wardrobes. Some hid their weapons in coal bins, false ceilings in wood piles or, if it worked out, in unused boilers and water tanks. A favorite trick was to place weapons in factories next to things that looked ominous, such as vats of acid, moving wheels, or moving drive shafts.

Explosives were usually buried around shrubbery, in planter boxes, or wherever a piece of soil was exposed. One Gestapo officer later claimed that if he had sent men around Paris to dig at random at the base of every tree and shrub during the height of the Resistance movement in 1943, they probably would have unearthed enough explosives to sink a British battleship. (Paris has a great number of parks, leading one to believe the claim was not completely without merit.)

Apparently, the most common method of caching weapons and ammo inside buildings in the city was to place them amongst the toilet plumbing or in the roof or attic. In such cases the caches were not large. When large numbers of weapons and explosives were required for a specific occasion, arrangements were made to ship them in from the countryside. After the odd patch of exposed soil within the inner city, the other common caching place was in garbage pails and refuse bins. Contemporary accounts written by French Resistance leaders mention garbage-can caching places with tiring frequency. (There was also a historical lesson in this experience. Today, one of the first evidence gathering procedures of BATF and DEA agents is to sift through a suspect's garbage. Apparently, these people learned at least this one thing from the Gestapo.)

• • • • •

An estimated 200,000 French men and women were killed in German concentration camps from 1941 through 1944. Of those that were actually involved in the Resistance (in reality, the movement claimed no more than 45,000 active members at any one time during the war, although the number of passive supporters was undoubtedly much higher), the most common violation was for possession and/or use of a weapon, including explosives. Caching was a most important element of the Resistance program, yet once the weapons were out of the cache, there was no practical means by which the carrier's intentions could be camouflaged. Caching itself was not particularly dangerous; carrying had great inherent risk. In that regard, little has changed.

CHAPTER THREE

Vietnam: A Hard-Learned Lesson on Caching

With the fall of the French at Dien Bien Phu on May 7, 1954, and the subsequent partitioning of Vietnam in Geneva on July 21, caching underwent its most thorough test as a modern combat strategy.

The U.S. government sent its best man, Edward Lansdale, to Vietnam with careful instructions to duplicate his recent success against the Huks in the Philippines. Lansdale implemented a caching strategy using planted "stay-behind groups" whose stated goal was to impede the Communist war machine in the northern sector as much as possible.

Ho Chi Minh implemented a similar strategy in the south. Perhaps because he sent ten thousand people south as compared to the three thousand the Americans sent north, and perhaps because the Communists were more brutal in terms of eliminating dissidents, Ho was more successful. Communist "stay-behinds" in the south, honed by twenty years of guerrilla warfare against the French, Japanese, and Chinese, and perhaps more studied in the lessons of the French Resistance, did a better job of implementing their strategy. After years of conflict, the North Vietnamese had become conditioned to cache weapons. At the first sign of trouble, their weapons went underground or underwater.

The French, and later the Americans, had a great advantage in terms of weapons, technology, and finance, while the Vietnamese had little more than cached weapons and a thoroughly indoctrinated, well-trained cadre of ground pounders. Prior to Vietnam, conventional wisdom held that one could not win a war without air superiority, including superior firepower. When it was all over, that wisdom, of course, had to be reexamined.

Steve Mattoon was one of the few Americans on the ground in Vietnam in the early days in 1962, just after a caching strategy had been implemented by both sides.

His six-man patrol moved as silently as smoke on the slippery yellow mud and low creeping vines in the gently rolling, forested northern area they were assigned to patrol. It was a classic example of mountainous Vietnam—not jungle, as many people expected, but an area populated with wrist-thick, oaklike bush and small grass. A heavy canopy of broadleaf teak and other upland oriental forest species towered over them. The canopy was a mixed blessing at best. To some extent, the leaves—some as large as a bucket lid—kept the sun off the men. It also trapped the stenchlike heat that rose in an ugly cloud from the forest floor.

Smoke from a lone hut or perhaps a village drifted up a little draw. It was barely perceptible except to those with keen noses. No wind or breeze was evident to transport the only sign of humans the men had come across for the last three hours. The smoke added to their discomfort, mostly because it warned them that the enemy was near.

They had been following a worn ridge line for an hour

Vietnam's forbidding, but beautiful, densely forested hills. The view here shows the kind of area Mattoon and his men were assigned to patrol.

or more. Mattoon waved the men on his left up the ridge and expertly placed them out to his right on either side of the draw. Mattoon knew that if they were not all careful, the high men on the sides of the finger drainage would soon find themselves dangerously out of contact as they headed downhill toward the smoke. He signaled again when they got down to a small trickle of water that fed a tangle of vegetation in the draw. Hopefully, training, his signals, and the natural survival instinct of the men would keep them out of trouble.

Thankfully, the mind blots out memories of the horrors of war that one can no longer bear to carry. Steve does not remember the name of his point man that day, although at the time they were reasonably close. From down the draw he heard the metallic clang of an automatic weapon. It sounded a bit odd, perhaps like a British Bren or maybe almost like the M14s his people carried. Steve didn't know immediately if it was hostile fire, but he was taking no chances. He could not see his point man below and had not seen him for five minutes or more.

Mattoon froze behind a large teak tree. From his left he heard an almost immediate string of aimed fire. It slapped and echoed up the draw. Three of his six-man patrol were visible. They were in a firefight, but so far it was very sporadic. A man high on the right signaled to move on down a bit.

Ever so cautiously, they moved down a bit until one of the men on the side hollered that the point man was down. Exercising as much caution as possible, the team moved quickly to their fallen comrade. It was only one of many that Mattoon would see. His first reaction was shock at how much blood was spilled from a single human container. Their point man was dead, hit at least twice in the body cavity.

In the draw to the left lay a crumpled Oriental dressed in short black pants and a tattered camouflage jacket. In this case, Mattoon was shocked again. The body lay twisted and broken. It seemed very small and childlike. "Perhaps the bad guys are using children as soldiers," he speculated.

Steve left three of his men up on the side of the draw while he examined his former point man. Flies were already starting to congregate. (Later in the war, he would understand that the appearance of flies so quickly was an indication of nearby civilization.)

They rolled the dead VC over and searched him for papers and weapons. The papers they found were unintelligible, due as much to the blood as the foreign language. The automatic weapon was an odd one. It looked much like a BAR except for the strange curved clip on top, a diminutive dog-leg wooden stock behind, and a strange barrel covered with cooling fins out ahead of the chamber area.

"A Type 99 Jap Nambu," one of the grunts grumbled. It was not a weapon Mattoon had seen before or had even expected to see. The weary GIs quickly broke two poles supporting a bean plant out of the ground for use as supports for their burden and dumped their load in the shelter half uncaringly. They placed the gun alongside their dead point man and continued down the hill.

Very shortly, the patrol carne to a small clearing containing a cluster of thatched houses surrounding a tiny rice paddy. The paddy, created by a high dike built across the little stream, created a field of an acre and a half at the most. Apparently the two crops of rice plus soybeans and squash that the little delta produced was enough for the four families in the area. They had no idea whether the hostile fire they had encountered originated from people in this village or if the people would all be friendly.

Mattoon and his men had no way of knowing if the people of the small village they had stumbled upon were the enemy or not . . . until they uncovered a number of weapons caches staked with Chinese C-4, a Chinese-made cannon, and other French, American, and Japanese weapons.

An old, bent white-bearded man approached in a kind of crouching, groveling posture, jabbering unintelligibly and seeming almost to laugh. The narrow, weed-lined path had never seen a vehicle other than some bicycles and perhaps a motor scooter or two. As the old man came, a few children's faces appeared at the far end of the path. Villagers and soldiers were equally suspicious. Perhaps the Vietnamese did not know what the shooting was all about, and perhaps they did.

Mattoon had finally established pretty good radio contact with headquarters. There was some confusion regarding their exact location. The village in which they found themselves was not on their map. "Check the village for weapons," ordered some distant voice.

More villagers appeared. Young men mixed with the old men and women gave Mattoon some cause for concern. Except for a machete or two stuck in their belts, no one seemed to be armed.

Cautiously at first, the five men started to check around the village. They estimated that it would be twenty minutes or more until the choppers arrived. Two of the thatched huts contained huge, wickerlike baskets full of raw, freshly harvested rice. The baskets were woven so tightly that Mattoon had to poke and prod to determine that they contained rice.

In another hootch, a fire on the floor smoldered and glowed on a section of blackened sheet steel. In an almost desultory fashion, Mattoon started probing in the thatch walls. Fortunately—or unfortunately, depending on the point of view—he happened to hit a small, three-pound cardboard box. The cardboard was heavily waxed. The entire packet was somewhat resilient, with a feel much like cheese.

Mattoon pulled out his belt knife and cut into the box. The material within looked somewhat like dirty American C-4. Unintelligible Chinese characters covered the sides of the container. He cut a small chunk off the rubbery block and threw it in the fire. It burned brightly for a brief time, giving off noticeable additional heat and light.

Excitedly, Mattoon raised his captain again on the radio. "We found some Chinese C-4," he shouted, "but the village is mostly a storage depot for rice. We are looking for additional weapons or explosives now."

"Tear those rice bins down and check inside," his captain ordered. "Check under the fires to see if there is any sign of tunneling. We'll send support in the choppers."

Just as Mattoon shut the radio down, one of the GIs came up with a worn old MAS 49 French submachine gun. "Got it out of the roof of that third house," he bragged. "It was woven into the thatch so it was really tough to find."

That did it. A thoroughly pissed off and concerned Mattoon got back on the radio requesting a full platoon of reinforcements, including interpreters to assist with the search. They obviously had stumbled across a Vietcong village from an unexpected direction.

In the granary, Mattoon took out his Gerber again, cutting the entire side out of one of the basketlike granaries. Rice spilled out all over the room and out of the sides of the building. From deep within the pile of rice he dug out a deep, orange wooden box. It was battered and beaten, still with the carry poles attached. The box held four brand new Czechoslovakian AK-47s, still in the grease. Excellent trading stock, Mattoon thought.

The second granary held four American M1 carbines. All showed signs of extensive use but had been carefully greased and wrapped with rags before being placed in the rice. Coated as they were, placed among a mountain of hygroscopic rice, the weapons were probably quite safe from the effects of the intense humidity and heat.

Ammunition was stored loose in hollow bamboo tubes leaning against the granary. All the villagers needed to do if they wanted to move their ammo was balance the pole on their shoulders and take off down the trail.

Mattoon believed that the poor villagers obeyed whoever was amongst them in the greatest force. At the time, the Americans were the most powerful force. (That night it might be the returned Vietcong.) They acted very humbly around the great white giants. For this reason, he recalls being somewhat dismayed and embarrassed by the vigor and enthusiasm of the newly arrived GIs and their Vietnamese interpreter as they tore into the houses with a great lack of care for the people's property.

Virtually every wall was stripped of its thatch. Mine detectors deployed around the village indicated that other buried caches existed. The closer the men looked, the more weapons caches they found. By the time the choppers started arriving, they had a respectable pile of hardware and explosives stacked in the clearing.

The greatest find occurred when Mattoon pulled up the steel plate on which one of the cook fires smoldered. Below it, a shaft dropped down about eight feet. He ran to the chopper for a flashlight. From the shaft he could see a tunnel running parallel to the ground about six feet deep. He called for the tunnel rat who came in with the choppers. The plan was for him to slide down the shaft and throw a gas grenade into the side tunnel.

Carefully, the man eased into the hole, but he did not have far to go. The tunnel dead-ended right about at the edge of the hut. But it was a bingo, nevertheless. Stored at the back was a brand new Chinese-made twin-barrel 23mm cannon.

Had the villagers had time to set all of their hardware up, the choppers never would have gotten in, and Mattoon would have lost most of his patrol. As it was, the patrol had apparently stumbled across a group of VC who were not yet ready for combat.

As a result of heated orders from the Vietnamese interpreter, all the village men were lined up for a bare-chested search. Some had obvious strap marks on their shoulders, indicating they had recently packed heavy loads for considerable distances. These men were bound with raw sisal and taken out by chopper. (Later in the war, such men were not so easily detained, but in

1962 everyone was still figuring out how to go about their business.)

Ammo for the big gun was stored in an identical cache under the second house. Like the machine gun captured earlier, many of the smaller weapons were of Japanese origin. After partition in 1954, North Vietnamese divers salvaged tons of supplies from coastal freighters sunk while resupplying the Japanese forces during World War II. Divers went down on free dives to sixty feet and, using weights and a simple air hose, brought up weapons, including explosives, from as far down as ninety feet.

Ton after ton of materiel was slowly and carefully salvaged by the Communists for use in the war against the French. At Dien Bien Phu, the Vietnamese acquired significant additional amounts of French and American weapons.

From 1954 until 1962, when they began to make their move, the Vietcong transported huge amounts of weapons and explosives to caches in the south. Locations of the caches were known by three-man cells, only one of whom knew the contact of the cell in the next village.

North Vietnamese regulars knew that aligned twigs, tied grass, or broken branches were signs that indicated a cache was near. Knowing basically how the caches were made, they would search around the area until the weapons they required were uncovered.

Eventually, thousands of tons of arms were moved south and cached. Americans had sophisticated radio communication nets, night vision devices, heavy artillery, and air support, but the Vietcong had weapons they hauled in on their backs either from the north or from the beaches, caching skills, dedication, and vast experience waging irregular warfare.

Along the coast and in the southern delta, weapons came in by small boat and sometimes freighters. Caches were placed inland a short distance, depending on local conditions. In the southern delta, caches were simply holes dug into high mounds and dikes where the corrosive coastal waters were unlikely to reach. As originally packed in China and Czechoslovakia, the weapons could be cached for six to eight months as long as they were not covered with water. Heavy grease and solid wooden crates provided reasonably good protection fur the short and intermediate run.

At times, the Vietcong scrounged shelter halves, plastic sheeting, nylon tarps, or corrugated tin to protect their caches. Mostly, however, they used woven mats and grass thatch to line their cache holes. Because of the incessant rain in some areas, it was as important to place a cover over the top of the boxes and cases as it was to place one under them, even though the weapons were buried several feet below the ground.

Ammunition was either cached in its original container or, for small arms, taken from the boxes and stored loose in wax-coated or shellacked bamboo tubes. Some of these tubes were four inches in diameter and could hide a considerable quantity of ammo or explosives. At times, full tubes were dropped in creeks or canals, but seldom was the ammo stored with the weapons.

Flooded rice paddies were a favorite caching place for the Vietcong. As the Americans became more sophisticated, they would run metal detectors around the dike of every paddy they came to. In numerous cases, they uncovered individual weapons coated with grease and wrapped in cloth under eighteen inches of water. The Vietcong responded by booby-trapping their caches and using the weapons as bait.

Steve Mattoon recalls the afternoon he fished a 120mm Russian motor tube out of a rice paddy. An American-style hand grenade placed as a booby trap threw its spoon next to him with a pop. Instantaneously, he threw himself over the dike, avoiding the explosion that was muffled to some extent by the mud and water.

When the Vietcong intended to cache weapons or ammo for the long term, they placed them in tied-off rubber inner tubes. Truck tubes could even protect larger crew-served weapons. In all likelihood, some caches in Vietnam today are probably still in good shape inside original rubber tubes.

GIs that were in Vietnam remember that it was impossible to keep an old inner tube around for any length of time. They always seemed to walk off (ending up, of course, in a hole in the ground, rice paddy, or stream, protecting a gun).

The Vietcong maintained both large regional caches and small personal hides. Both were frequently uncovered by GIs. Perhaps because there were so many, virtually every GI who went on patrol in Vietnam eventually found weapons of some sort.

In addition to rice paddies, cemeteries were good places for the Vietcong to cache weapons. At the time of Tet in 1968, ground observers believed that most of the weapons brought into the inner cities were transported in coffins. Some GIs who fought their way through that one believed that as many as five hundred bogus funerals were organized in Saigon alone.

Burial grounds were high and dry, and the exact place where each coffin full of arms was interred could be recorded on a visible grave marker. Both GIs and Saigon government soldiers tried to uncover weapons caches in cemeteries, but they usually came up short because there was so much other metal buried with the average Vietnamese corpse. Mine detectors gave enough readings to keep an entire brigade busy digging for years.

Toward the end of the war, almost all large caches were placed in the extensive Vietcong tunnel network. Some of these tunnels were so elaborate that they not only contained crew-served weapons, but also entire weapons factories, as well as hospitals, prisons, and large food storage areas.

In these instances, weapons, RPGs, and mortar rounds were going out of the caches as fast as they were coming in. More and more individual Vietnamese decided to take up arms as it became increasingly obvious who was going to win the war. In that regard, their strategy evolved from caching to hiding. Increasingly, ground actions were supported by mortar fire. Mortar rounds that came down through Cambodia were kept briefly—only until enough were accumulated for an engagement—and then sent out for use.

Toward the end, finding caches was no longer a high priority for GIs. They picked up what they found, but often the weapons were not even taken back to camp. Many grunts reported digging a small hole, piling in the weapons and ammo, and then firing a block of C-4 to destroy them.

Edward Lansdale's plan to spread havoc in the north by using caches and "stay-behinds" came to naught. Apparently, too few stay-behinds became active, and the general population in the north did not support them.

In the south, however, caching really worked. After things got rolling in 1962, anyone who wanted a weapon could get one—many times in the exact make and model and from the country of choice.

CHAPTER FOUR

Caching and You

Ray Wilson travels often on business to Washington, D.C., As a professional geologist, he feels it is important to keep in touch with members of his profession in the National Geological Survey Office. Taxpayers cover his travel expenses, so Dr. Wilson can think of no valid monetary reason for not taking the trips as often as possible.

On one such trip several years back, Wilson, the admittedly small-town boy, decided to stop at a drugstore on Wisconsin Avenue, in the heart of Georgetown, at about 10:00 P.M. On his way into the store from the public sidewalk, he found it necessary to wade through a number of D.C.'s finest, most persistent, obnoxious panhandlers. Being from a part of the western United States where these sorts of people virtually do not exist, Wilson was not equipped to deal with the situation in which he found himself.

Sensing his fear, the moochers pressed him vigorously, ignoring other potential donors. Two of them stood together in the middle of the sidewalk, effectively blocking his way into the store. Somehow these people felt Wilson owed them money, a claim they pressed even more vocally and physically when they realized he was uncertain about the situation. Once inside the store, the now very shaken Wilson tried to persuade the store manager that he had been the victim of a rough, dangerous encounter. He pleaded with the manager to call the police.

"They won't respond even if I do call," the manager explained patiently. "What are you, some kind of hick? District police only look into holdups of more than five hundred dollars, shootings, or major drug deals."

"But I can't go back out there again," Wilson pleaded passionately. "They will tear me to pieces."

"If they do tear you to pieces, then the police will investigate, but I suggest you wait here for fifteen or twenty minutes and then leave with several other customers," the manager persisted.

Finally that's what he did. Wilson walked out of the store with a group of Washington natives who knew how to deal with panhandlers. On the way back to his hotel room, Wilson vowed never to let such an incident happen again. Lesser people might have settled for a relatively wimpy can of tear gas or some similar device, but not Wilson. He was an exploration geologist, accustomed to wild and wooly situations.

I got involved when Wilson asked me to sell him a small handgun. In the course of the sale, he told me about the incident in Georgetown and explained how he planned to deal with this sort of thing in the future. It was interesting to keep track of events as they unfolded.

When Wilson flew into our nation's capital, he always went through National Airport. From there he took a taxi directly to the Key Bridge Marriott where, for reasons of access, cost, and comfort, he liked to stay. Washington, D.C., is packed full of hotels, but for those who have not stayed there, the Key Bridge Marriott is characterized by larger than normal gardens and sundry strips of shrubbery, many of which are inside the hotel along various courts and walks that are out of sight from any but those few guests who use them.

At the time this incident occurred, the airlines did not fluoroscope or otherwise examine checked baggage to any great extent. Wilson put his pistol and a box of ammo in his suitcase and sent it on through to National Airport. As was his custom, he stayed at the same Marriott outside of Georgetown.

However, this time Wilson retrieved the pistol from his suitcase and carried it with him in an ankle holster as he went about his business in D.C. He knew which buildings were protected by metal detectors, so he would leave the pistol in his briefcase with a security officer when he went through a security system.

When ready to leave the city, Wilson inspected the two clips, wrapped the pistol and ammo in rust-inhibiting paper, and sealed both in quality plastic bags he had purchased just for this occasion. After sealing up the bags, he buried them about twelve inches deep in one of the Marriott flower beds. He picked a place where there was a distinctive mark on the wall to facilitate finding his cache the next time he came to D.C.

Whenever Wilson arrives in D.C. now, he simply retrieves his piece, performs any necessary cleaning, and goes about Washington equal to any three muggers. Today, Wilson maintains significantly increased peace of mind while moving around from place to place in the big city. (Someday a Bernard Goetz-type incident may occur, and Mr. Wilson will fault me for putting his account in print.)

By caching in a common area such as a flower bed, Wilson does not have to worry about requesting the same

This Walther PPK with extra magazines and a box of ammo has been buried in a flower bed at a Washington, D.C., hotel for nearly fifteen years. The owner carries the weapon for protedion whenever he does business in the capital city.

Walther PPK double-bagged for burial.

room in the Marriott every time he comes to town. Above-ground locations might work, but the chances of having his pistol discovered in the course of routine maintenance or repair would be much greater.

Recently, airline search procedures have become more sophisticated. Today, Wilson might not get away with carrying a pistol through in checked baggage. In all probability, he would have to smuggle a pistol in using a private automobile or public ground transportation, such as a bus or train. Since he launched his personal protection program, virtually every criminal in Washington, D.C.—probably some panhandlers included—has upgraded his weapons. Wilson believes that anyone without a sidearm in that city is at a real disadvantage.

Caching a pistol in crime-plagued Washington, D.C., is an excellent example of a modern-day self-defense strategy. In the burgeoning struggle for survival, this is one practical application for caching that may be useful to a number of citizens. But it is only one of several.

Investment

Back in the mid-'30s, when the Federal Firearms Act was enacted, a close friend who happened to be the sheriff in Tippecanoe County, Indiana, bought three 1928 Navy-model Thompson submachine guns for private use. Because of the new law, popular opinion held that these sort of guns were just about worthless. He purchased them for thirty dollars apiece. He coated the guns with grease inside and out, put them in a rough box built of heavy cyprus planks, and buried them in the ground for long-term storage.

Because of the limited technology of that era, he found he had to dig the Thompsons up from time to time to be sure they remained in good shape. They kept well over the years, due largely to the ideal location in which he chose to place the cache. Tippecanoe County is characterized by well-drained, sandy soil. By avoiding swamps and bog holes, he was able to keep the weapons absolutely rust-free until the time came to sell them.

My friend the sheriff retired in 1958, and his wife contracted cancer in early 1964. He dug the weapons up for the last time and took them to town to sell. As it worked out, they were an excellent investment for the man, having appreciated many times over. He secured top dollar for weapons that were virtually unavailable from any other source.

In this instance, weapons caching went beyond being a self-preservation plan and became a valid investment strategy. Should semiautomatic weapons—including so-called assault rifles—suddenly be banned, those who have them and are willing and able to put them in the ground

Burying your semiautos now, before they are banned, goes beyond self-defense or self-preservation. It is a valid financial investment strategy.

Cache ammunition in smaller tubes alongside your weapons. Since ammo rarely, if ever, decreases in value, it is a good investment. And it may not always be as freely available as it is today.

for a few years will later find their investment has doubled or tripled. Already we have seen common AK-47s and AR-15s go from a little over four hundred dollars to a thousand dollars or more.

Ammo is an excellent item to consider when looking at investment caching. It keeps as well or better in a cache than weapons, and because it is consumed rapidly under some circumstances, it is not nearly as easily replaced as one might initially suppose. Gun nuts who are accustomed to popping down to the local gun shop for a fresh supply of powder, bullets, or loaded rounds should give this concept some serious thought.

Early in the surplus military weapons era I purchased two million rounds of ammo on behalf of a firearms shop for which I worked. The lot included 9mm Parabellum, 8mm Japanese pistol, 7.62mm NATO, 8mm Lebel, 8mm Mauser, 6.5 x 55 Swedish Mauser, and some

6.5 x 54R Dutch ammo. We paid two cents per round on the average, and I was certain we would never get our forty thousand dollars back out of the deal, much less turn a profit. However, when surplus weapons started to sell in large numbers, we priced most of the calibers at ten dollars per hundred rounds for the first six months, then twelve dollars and fifteen dollars until it was all sold.

Some calibers sold better than others, but we made excellent money on the entire lot. It was only one of many lots of ammo we purchased for resale. Through the years we always scraped together enough cash to purchase any odd or surplus ammo available. At one time, we had at least $100,000 tied up in .25-, .32-, and .41-caliber rimfire ammo as well as less exotic numbers such as .303 Savage, 6mm Lee Navy, .25-20 single shot, .30 Remington, .33 Winchester, and many others.

These 8rnm Mauser rounds, made in 1914, have been cached since 1964. Despite the corrosion seen on the left round, only one in fifty fails to fire.

Right now, while cheap surplus ammo is still available, I might suggest that it would be a "no-brainer" to buy up a large supply of the more commonly used calibers and put it underground until the time when it becomes scarce. Ammo virtually never goes down in price.

In my personal cache, I have some surplus 8mm Mauser ammo, manufactured in Turkey in 1914, which was originally part of a two-million-round order placed in 1962. It came to us in sealed cans. Other than the small amount I blasted away for fun, I left the ammo in the sealed containers and resealed it in cache tubes. Now, more than seventy-five years after its manufacture, the ammo still fires reasonably well. About one round in fifty will not fire, but since it is mostly blasting ammo manufactured under questionable circumstances, I don't consider this to be an insurmountable problem.

Personal Protection

Weapons can be cached for isolated circumstances when personal safety is threatened and a sure method of self-defense is needed to provide peace of mind, and they can also be cached for investment purposes. But for most people, weapons caching provides safe, longterm storage of their best means of personal protection.

As laws change and rules are promulgated by state and national legislators, the need for caching may become especially pressing. Citizens of California and New Jersey who wish to remain at least on an equity base with criminals, or who have expensive guns they do not wish to throw onto an uncertain market, are already victims of a force that may be a harbinger of things to come throughout this nation.

In other places, gun nuts with large collections of guns and ammo may be victims of this force as well. A law-abiding gun owner may thwart the robbery of his home, only to be harassed unmercifully by the media. Who wants to read about himself in the paper— **"Local man found with dozens of guns, thousands of rounds of ammo."** No matter that there were only nine guns and that three were single-shot 410s that you bought for your kids and that "thousands of rounds" is only four or five cartons of 22s all purchased at a dollar per box. The media will fry gun owners if they get any chance at all. Just the fact that a gun nut has several weapons and more than a handful of ammo is more than enough cause for the media to come down very hard on him. Though our hobby constitutes no threat to anyone except criminals, every gun owner is held in contempt and suspicion.

Gun owners who foresee themselves in these types of uncomfortable circumstances may wish to consider caching all of the weapons they do not plan to use on a frequent basis. Those who do it now, under relatively easy, unpressured circumstances, may be the real winners in the long run. They will have enough time to think through their caching program adequately so that they can do it right.

Most really clever, innovative cachers require time to develop their programs. Especially for city dwellers with few burying options, caching done under duress is never as good as long-term plans that may involve some sophisticated masonry or carpenter work involving rerouting water pipes and so on.

Many inner-city gun owners fear that possessing weapons will, ironically, single them out as targets for common criminals (as opposed to official criminals), who either want weapons for their own use or know where they can sell all the quality weapons and ammo they can steal to people with all the money to buy them. Preventing your weapons from being stolen is another reason for caching, and it is a worthy one.

• • • • •

You can build clever hides that allow you to look at your weapons from time to time. You may still wish to tape a box of ammo to the bottom of a dresser drawer or the lid of the toilet tank, but putting the bulk of your guns in a good cache now, when the time is available to do it right—before the thieves break in and while personal protection is still an option—may be the smartest decision you, as a prudent gun owner, can make. If nothing else, your cache can be viewed as an investment that will pay great dividends in one way or another.

CHAPTER FIVE

Modern Caching Technology

Since World War II, remarkable new advances in caching technology have drastically altered almost every aspect of strategic weapons storage. Caching equivalents to atomic warfare make it possible to hide weapons under virtually any environmental circumstance. It is now possible to store your guns in a sewer, a lake, a running stream, a vat of acid, a freezer, a chimney, or a host of similar places that the bad guys are either unlikely or unwilling to think about. This is the good news.

The bad news is that the other side also has some fantastic new technology to work with. Some of the space-age gizmos they use are so good that the cacher must use all of his wit and intellect to keep the cache intact. It's the age-old rule of measure and countermeasure, of technology ratcheting each side up in a kind of lock step. Yet the new technology we have presents opportunities unheard of even a few years ago. It would, for instance, be advisable under some circumstances to place your cache tube inside a furnace closure next to a firebox after wrapping it in a space blanket. There are many other locations around the home or farm and at the workplace where the bad guys either will not look or will be reluctant to search thoroughly. A farm silo or the bottom of a large granary are excellent choices. It would take weeks and tens of thousands of dollars for searchers to empty these bins on the outside chance that they might contain a cache. In the case of a silo, it might be dangerous for the authorities to search it because of dangerous gases produced inside.

However, septic tanks and sewers, which appear at first to offer some of the most interesting possibilities, do not in reality have much to recommend them. Recently, the DEA, FBI, and federal marshals have pumped virtually every septic tank they encountered at places in the country where they were searching for drugs or munitions. It has been just about their first order of business when searching for contraband. Perhaps it is a logical extension of the Nazi experience of uncovering caches in refuse containers, but at this point it seems like good advice not to cache in septic tanks or garbage receptacles. Bomb squads look first into garbage cans and wastebaskets, leaving one to conclude these sorts of locations are not particularly secure.

For the purposes of this analysis, one must assume that there is a great difference between large weapons caches and hiding a weapon or two in your apartment. Subsequent chapters will cover hiding personal weapons. Many caching and hiding techniques are similar, but there is a difference—in psychology if not mechanics. To be successful, the cacher must understand this and be able to distinguish between the two.

Modern caching techniques are not particularly difficult when viewed in their component parts. The techniques can be exacting but are not difficult to master. Sloppy execution will lead to poor results, while the opposite is certainly true—careful execution will lead to excellent results.

My first experience with a weapons cache was much the same as that of the sheriff from Tippecanoe County. It was a long time ago, but as I remember, we took a GI-surplus wooden box that once housed three 3.5-inch bazooka rockets, disassembled our weapons, stacked the various parts neatly in the box, and filled it up with molten grease. We purchased the grease from a farm supply store in five-gallon pails. I believe it took two full pails to cover everything completely.

Since many military-type weapons have limited amounts of wood to deteriorate, they tend to store well. The laser sight must be removed and placed in a smaller cache tube.

We removed the wooden stocks from the weapons and stored them in another location. Wood will deteriorate in grease much faster than steel, we reasoned, but this was not a particularly wise decision. Anyone who noticed the stocks would have suspected a nefarious weapon or two might be lurking somewhere near as well. Modern military weapons are seldom constructed using wooden stocks, but not all of us have the privilege of caching the most modern weapons. Some citizens, for instance, may feel harassed to the point that they simply wish to cache a superaccurate bolt action rifle. Today I would leave the wood with the metal, assuming that both will last a minimum of twenty years in an airtight container.

Another problem we had with storing the parts separately was that some of the pieces were misplaced. After a time, we didn't know for sure if they were in one cache or another. On one occasion we returned to a cache after a great number of years only to discover that a key part was irretrievably lost. From then on, only complete weapons packages went into a single cache.

Even in a military context, disassembling a weapon to save space may not be a particularly good idea. Unless the disassembly is very basic, small parts may be misplaced or hidden in the grease coating. Removing the stock from a Thompson or splitting a Schmeisser in half, for instance, might be okay, but removing a scope from a rifle to be cached is often of questionable value (although sometimes it must be done).

How does one reassemble and rezero a previously cached rifle with its scope? Test-firing semiautomatic weapons attracts quite a lot of attention. Rezeroing a scoped rifle over larger distances may be out of the question for some city dwellers. (Maybe that's why the hero in many spy stories is never successfully shot by the villain sniper.) In occupied France, the situation became so tough that replacements for fallen Resistance members could not be trained with firearms. They simply had no place to practice or to sight-in weapons. This situation may seem unlikely in the United States, but I'll bet few owners will be taking their semiautos to the range to practice in California.

Modern caching equipment roughly breaks down into the following essential categories.

Plastic Container

Since most caches are placed in the ground in a vertical position, it is best to use standard round plastic plumbing pipe. Purchasing sections of pipe from the local plumber will not be a problem since they sell dozens of similar items to hundreds of people each day. When the Bureau of Alcohol, Tobacco and Firearms (BATF) people inquire, the clerk will have no recollection of what you purchased. If a question does come up, tell the people at the plumbing shop that you intend to construct a map tube or a fishing pole holder.

Cache tubes must always be placed in the ground vertically. Horizontal tubes expose too much surface area to sensitive metal detectors. Always bury the tube so the top is at least one foot below the surface.

Many army/navy surplus stores carry polyurethane plastic barrels about the size of fifty-five-gallon steel drums that are intended for caching. They are thick and tough with an adequate screw-type lid through which most weapons could be passed. Though these barrels are fine for caching food and medicine, they are not recommended for weapons. Their overall width, plus the huge mass of steel they might contain, make them extremely easy targets for modern metal detectors.

Use the four-, six-, or eight-inch diameter SDR (Sanitary, Drain, Refuse) pipe found at virtually any full-service plumbing shop. There is a lightweight and a heavy grade of four-inch pipe. Use only the heavyweight material if a four-inch cache tube is adequate. Six- and eight-inch tubing come only in heavy and extra-heavy grades. Inexperienced cachers will try to get by on smaller tubes

Installing the end cap on a four-inch cache tube. Most cachers find that four-inch tubes are too small for anything except ammunition and magazines.

A four-inch cache tube will hold a tremendous quantity of ammunition.

A new sixty-inch section of eight-inch cache tube, ready to be filled with weapons.

initially because they are easier to find and much cheaper, but almost everyone eventually uses eight-inch pipe for their cache tubes. There is a high-pressure, eight-inch plastic pipe called a "blue boot," but it far exceeds the needs—and perhaps the pocketbook—of most cachers. The wall thickness on blue boot pipe is almost three-quarters of an inch.

A section of eight-inch plastic pipe will hold quite a load of weapons. Count on placing at least two full-sized rifles, four assault rifles, four or five pistols, and dozens of magazines in a single eight-inch tube. (Enough, my friends claim, to start a revolution in Central America.)

It is best to have the tube cut at a length of sixty inches. This way, even the longest semiautomatic weapons will fit inside the tube, and the parts will have an opportunity to settle into the lower end, farther from the probing eye of a metal detector.

Common eight-inch slip-type end cap used with a grease closure on a cache tube.

Heavy-duty, four-inch SDR pipe retails for about $.95 per foot, six-inch pipe for about $1.55, and eight-inch, the most common cache tube size, for about $4.15. Some small stores must special-order eight-inch pipe and will want you to purchase an entire ten-foot section.

Various threaded plugs can be purchased for the tubes, but usually the best and cheapest are simple slipon end caps. Threaded fittings are theoretically easier to get into and more secure, but this is not always true out in the field. Threaded caps clog with dirt and are often as difficult as slip caps to remove. They are no more impervious to water under most circumstances than a simple, inexpensive grease-sealed end cap.

Plain end caps for four-inch pipe cost about $1.50, six-inch caps $6.90, and eight-inch slip caps $21. Female adapters into which a plug could be threaded cost roughly $5.25 for a four-inch pipe, $16.20 for a six-inch pipe, and

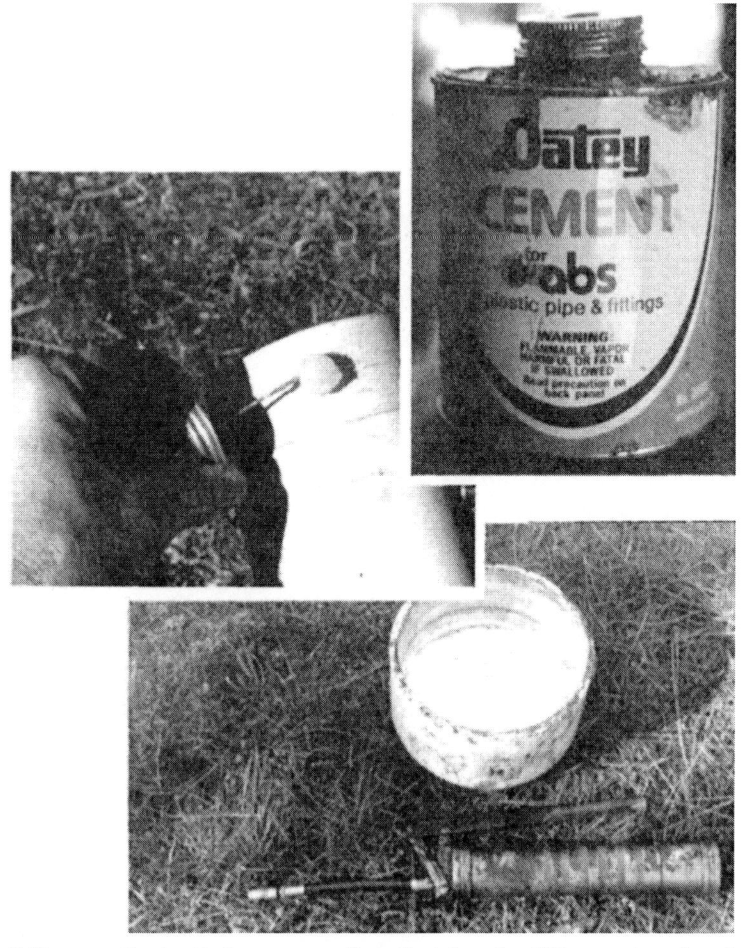

Top Left: Permanently glue the lower cap on the cache tube using ABS cement purchased from a plumbing supply house. Top Right: ABS cement used to attach caps to cache tubes. Bottom: Eight-inch slip-type cap for cache tube with grease gun used to attach cap.

are not even made for eight-inch pipe. Plugs for the two available sizes are $2 and $5 each.

Whatever closure system you choose, you will cement one cap on the lower end of your cache tube per-

A hand grease gun is used to apply common lube grease to the end of an eight-inch cache tube prior to placement of the end cap.

Grease sealant being applied to the inside of the end cap.

Placing slip cap onto cache tube.

manently. There is no reason to install expensive fittings on the end of a pipe that will be in the ground. Use heavy pump grease to coat the end of the pipe and the cap on the top access end. After you've glued the bottom cap on, you can check the seal to determine whether the tube will hold pressure by pushing a cap onto the top end. If there is a leak, the cap will pop off the top of the tube right away. If it is a good seal, air pressure will build up in the tube, preventing the cap from settling on the end of the pipe initially, but once the air pressure equalizes, you'll be able to push it on. (If the cap absolutely cannot be pushed on the tube because of the air pressure, drill a small hole in the cap to allow the trapped air to escape. Pressurizing the tube provides

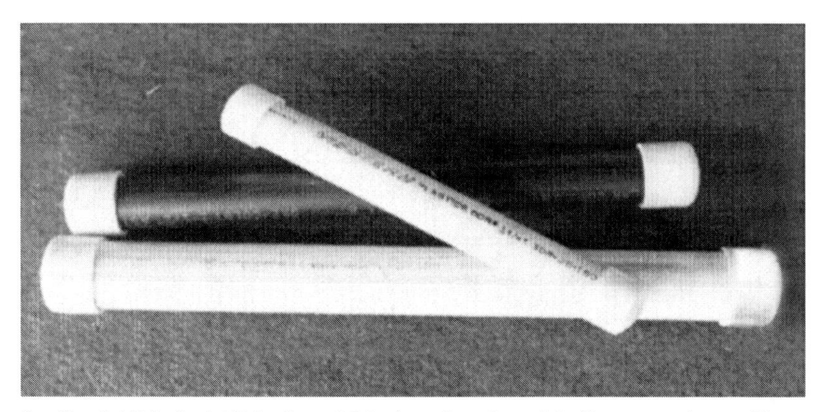

Smaller 1 1/4-inch, 1 1/2-inch, and 2-inch cache tubes with slip-type end caps. These are useful for storing scopes, ammo, laser sights, and other small parts within the full-size tube.

an additional barrier against moisture. Do not drill a hole to relieve this pressure unless it is absolutely necessary.) At times it is very difficult to pry these pressurized caps off the tubes once they equalize and "set up." I use a small hammer to tap them off or a piece of two-by-four as a pry. Some cachers use standard PVC glue to place a small handle on the cap so it can be pulled and rotated to open.

If you feel you must remove the scope from a rifle to be cached, it is always best to place it in its own internal plastic pipe container. This isn't the best situation, but it is way ahead of anything else if you must cache a scoped rifle.

For all practical purposes, these sealed plastic tubes are impervious to the elements. Whatever is stored in them today would certainly emerge in fine shape if dug up in the year 2001. If you are positive the cache will remain in place ten years or more, it is advisable to seal both ends. In this case, if you wanted to use the enclosed weapons in the year 2001, you would have to saw the pipe open with a carpenter's saw.

Rust-Preventative Coating

Treating weapons that are stored within an airtight cache tube is a matter of some debate among the caching fraternity. Most cachers agree that it is best to coat them with either regular grease or special oil made to prevent rust and other deterioration. Some simply cache their weapons as they came off the rack.

Conoco makes a product called "Cotton-Pickers Spindle Grease," a special rust preventative that protects metal parts as well as or better than anything else around. The product is a thin grease, almost liquid at room temperature. It sells for about twenty-five dollars per five-gallon pail. In most sections of the country it would be necessary to special order it from a local petroleum products distributor.

Metal parts on weapons can be coated with this material, and while it does not harm wood in the short or intermediate run, it may deteriorate it after very prolonged storage. The grease is thin enough that it may all run off into the bottom of the tube if the ground warms a bit. Apparently, enough would remain to control rust for at least ten to fifteen years.

Cachers can also use the less exotic technique of applying a thin coating of regular lube grease to their weapons. The coating can be as thick or thin as one feels is appropriate. Some surplus shops still have the odd bucket of inexpensive Cosmoline around. This material, if one can find it, will do the job very nicely. Expect to pay about seventy-five cents to a dollar per pound for grease and about thirty-five cents a pound for surplus Cosmoline.

Invariably, the question arises—why not pour the tube solid with grease? It can be done, but it is a very expensive procedure. While it is also very effective, it probably is not as effective as blister packing (covered in another chapter). Also, solid-packed cache tubes are so heavy that it is difficult to carry them to their burying place, and it is impossible to remove or inspect the weapons in the tube once cached. Still, caches under these circumstances are extremely stable. There is no way of knowing, but I suspect the contents would remain in good shape for at least a thousand years. If the cap were sealed, the tube could be placed on the ocean floor and still be expected to last a long, long time.

As an added precaution, you can cover the weapons with grease or special rust-preventative oil and then wrap them in Valpon rust-preventative paper. (Undoubtedly, you can purchase this paper, but I do not know where. My best, most reliable source is a friend who works in an automobile parts store and saves sheets of it for me.) Wrap this paper tightly around the weapon and/or the parts packages. The grease on the weapons will tend to hold the paper.

Silica Gel

As a last measure to control any errant moisture in the tubes, you might want to place at least two ounces of silica gel in a sixty-inch tube that's eight inches in diameter (less for smaller tubes). Silica gel is available from chemical supply warehouses for about five dollars a pound, or you can ask your druggist to save the surplus packets and caps from the bottles of pills he unpacks. Collect the surplus once a month and you will be surprised at how much you accumulate at no cost. Be sure to use silica gel as a desiccant as opposed to the other common chemical used for this purpose, calcium chloride, which is a strong salt that corrodes metal quickly under the right circumstances. Place the silica gel in a cardboard container in which you have punched numerous small holes. Throw the cardboard container into the tube right before sealing it up.

If the cache is poured solid with grease or the weapons are plastic sleeved, there is, of course, no reason to use a desiccant. Most experienced cachers report that use of silica gel is a nice gesture but not really important in terms of safe storage. If the weapons are only lightly greased, silica gel might be useful, but usually it seems to contribute little.

The most important step is to seal the tube thoroughly after it is in place and the parts are inserted. Use generous amounts of grease around the cap mouth, and be certain the air seal is maintained unless you elect to seal the tube permanently. Where the cache tube is located dictates how completely it must be sealed. Tubes placed in swamps, stream beds, lakes, storm sewers, or acid baths must be completely sealed. In these cases, you probably should figure on gluing the cap in place. (In spite of the expense and difficulty, marshes, streams, and lakes are excellent cache locations because searchers have a tough time using their sophisticated electronic-detection devices. Under these circumstances, they may assume an errant reading because to do otherwise would create a huge amount of work in disagreeably cold and wet conditions.)

Soil Auger

Correctly burying a cache tube is something of an art; it can also be tedious and expensive. During the early '80s, I lived for a time in a very posh inner-city condominium. I felt it was important that I set up a cache, but obviously I could not do so with any safety within the building. After contemplating the situation for several months, I decided to bury it in one of the many shrub-

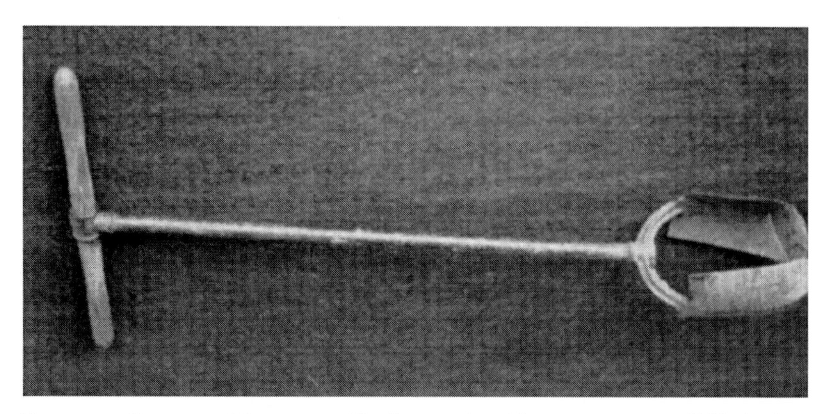

Common soil augers of the type used by farmers to set fence posts are available in sizes ranging from six to twelve inches. You should use a twelve-inch auger to place most cache tubes. A twelve-inch auger will dislodge an incredible pile of loose material from its hole, so plan ahead for disposal.

A three-quarter-inch common pipe connects the digging head of a soil auger with its turning handle.

bery beds surrounding the building. Burying a cache tube necessitates the use of a soil auger. (It can be done with a shovel, but not very well.)

Soil augers, used by farmers to set fence posts, are sold in six- through twelve-inch sizes at nursery and farm supply stores for about forty dollars each. Regular caliper-type post hole digging tools are generally inadequate for the job of setting a cache tube because they will not dig down deep enough.

Soil augers are connected to the turning handle on top by a piece of three-quarter-inch pipe. The device will dig down about four feet. Angering the soil out of the hole is not difficult under most circumstances. At four feet, you must splice in an additional three-foot section of three-quarter-inch pipe using a common pipe union. Thus equipped, you can go down another two feet or more, deep enough to place a five-foot tube one foot underground.

Dig down into the ground five to seven feet, depending on the length of the cache tube. Placing soil on the tarp (right) helps keep the visual impact of installing the tube to a minimum.

After digging down four feet with the soil auger, splice in a three-foot section of pipe so that the hole can be bored down deep enough to hold the cache.

At the condo, it was a fine, bright winter day in the desert. I put on an old pair of bib overalls and went out to the hedge bed early one morning when I knew the manager was out of town and started digging like it was the most natural thing in the world. Nobody recognized me, and I was able to dig a twelve-inch hole down to the required depth. (At times, in gravelly soil, this is not as easy as it sounds.) A twelve-inch hole produces a huge amount of loose material, all of which I placed in burlap bags and loaded in my car. I told one curious resident that I was taking soil samples, and that was my only inquiry.

After the hole was completed, I slid the tube into the space, covered the hole with dirt, and rescattered the wood chips from under the shrubbery back over the new excavation. (Tubes placed in the ground using this method are pretty much permanent. Soil settles back in around them, making the tube virtually impossible to pull. It helps to file a bevel on the lower cap so that the tube slides easier, but even this does not provide much assistance. Tubes placed in wet, marshy conditions can be pulled with a bit more ease, but even these require quite a bit of work to retrieve intact.)

Later, during the crisp dark of evening, I crept out of the condo with my cache items. The shrubbery hid me, or I could have been in a lot of trouble. Quickly, I uncovered the tube with my hands and slid the cache items down safely below. They resided there safe and sound until1985 when I moved back to the country. It is helpful to place a disk attached to a dowel rod or rope in the bottom of the tube so that you can retrieve small items more easily (assuming you will move items in and out of the cache). Otherwise, you may have to fish out the small parts that fell to the bottom with a magnet.

Vertically installed cache tubes are very difficult to relocate. It took great effort to dig out this one, which was in the ground for eight years.

As this story demonstrates, people living in cities will have a great many more problems successfully locating a cache than those in the country. In this regard, modern-day Americans are no different than members of the French Resistance or the Vietcong. If you will but look at it from the perspective of the authorities, you will realize the range of options in the country are far greater than in the city. Sophisticated searchers at my condo would have realized that the flower beds were the only place I could have cached and may have found them with sophisticated metal detectors. However, it was the only option I had in those circumstances.

My favorite caching spot in the country is right in the middle of a well-traveled gravel road. Pick a spot twenty feet from a large, distinctive tree and bore down with the auger. In spring, the digging is very easy after the initial three or four inches of gravel are turned aside. The county government did me a favor at one cache site when they blacktopped the road, permanently sealing in my cache tube. That cache will probably be there when I turn ninety. Certainly no one will find it, and my guess is that the contents will be in excellent shape.

If possible, bury chunks of steel in the vicinity of your cache-pieces of scrap, large bolts and nuts, whatever will confuse metal detectors. Place them in clustered locations away from the cache to create the illusion that the cache is somewhere near. GIs in Vietnam reported that they found metal with their mine detectors in every cemetery. They also reported that large numbers of weapons were almost always hidden in these same cemeteries. Yet, perhaps because of social problems and plain old laziness, they often did not dig in the cemeteries where they got good readings. Unless the authorities are powerfully motivated by other sources of information, such as informants, witnesses, observed traffic to the cache area, and so forth, they will probably not work their way through a large number of false readings.

If the cache tube is stored under an incinerator, outdoor barbecue, or any other place where heat may be a problem, place a piece of tinfoil or heavy reflective paper over the top of the tube. In some cases, it may be appropriate to wrap the entire tube in reflective paper (from a lumber yard) or in an old space blanket.

In summary, build a good cache tube out of SDR pipe and suitable caps, coat the weapons with rust preventative grease, wrap them in rust preventative paper, place them in the tube, and drop in a packet of silica gel if necessary. Seal the tube well and stand it vertically in a deep hole.

Be aware that clever cache locations weigh heavily in the equation and that military-type weapons store far better than commercial ones (especially if the commercial types have extensive intricate woodwork and glass sights). Scopes, if you must remove them, should be sealed in their own separate container but placed in the tube with their intended rifles. Wood, leather, and canvas keep poorly in caches over the long haul.

Start developing a cache plan early so that the best location—whether it is a swamp, storm sewer, flower bed, road, or incinerator—can be chosen. Keep in mind that as a result of the modern materials available to cachers at plumbing supply shops, virtually any location can be utilized.

CHAPTER SIX

Caching vs. Hiding

Most regular practitioners of the art of caching eventually find that their day-to-day activities are focused on hiding their weapons as opposed to caching. In a tough, military-type context, where the user must keep at least some of his tools reasonably handy, this is extremely common. This is precisely the trend that both the French Resistance and the Vietcong experienced. Hiding was, for these people, the art of keeping a few weapons and a relatively small number of rounds of ammunition close at hand for immediate use, whereas caching was done on a more regional basis and usually involved a larger number of weapons and explosives.

Caching is semipermanent. Hiding is a temporary measure undertaken mostly for the immediate personal convenience of the end user. Gun owners in New York and Chicago would most likely engage in hiding activities, while those in California and New Jersey would most likely cache. Of course, the intensity with which the authorities might seek out gun owners also enters the equation. Caching is generally much safer and less likely to lead to seizure.

Most gun nuts have hidden a weapon or two around their homes. Strategic caching, however, is a new concept to most people. Most people have problems differentiating between the two. There is a difference, however, and you must be able to separate the two functions in your own mind. You now have a decision to make, but the tools are at hand if you decide to cache.

Some modern caching techniques have crossover applications for hiders, and there are innovative new hiding methods that may be of interest to gun owners who do not feel they must cache at this time. Weapon owners must decide for themselves to what extent they are threatened and plan accordingly.

In several recent situations, it was obvious that federal marshals searching the homes of suspects deliberately attempted to tear the dwelling up as much as possible in order to coerce the property owner into giving in to their threats. In these circumstances, destruction is often not limited to what can be done with crow bar and hammer. A national news magazine recently carried a story regarding federal marshals who, in Nazi-like fashion, rented a large backhoe to assist them with the chore of tearing off a chunk of some poor citizen's home. Perhaps our marshals took their training from GIs returning from Vietnam, where entire villages were often burned in a search for weapons.

Assuming you are willing to suffer silently through a destructive search and/or maintain a low profile so that the authorities are unsure when they search, there are several modern hiding concepts that have promise. They are not foolproof, but they are helpful.

Most home hiding techniques are costly and difficult to implement. Probably the simplest is to take your heat-ing system apart and hide a weapon way up in the ducts. This will foil metal detectors, and the piece will keep nicely in the controlled atmosphere.

Be extremely cautious when implementing this or any other technique within a house or apartment. Repaint any nails and screws that are damaged, and keep any natural metal screws in nice, bright condition. Customs inspectors who search vessels for illegal drugs look first for screws that have been burred or that have paint that has been scarred.

Another excellent location is under the bathroom vanity between the riser or the sink cabinet and the floor. Again, the location is a good one because the pipes and faucets provide a sufficient mass of metal to confuse most metal detectors.

Most vanities are screwed into the wall at the rear of the cabinet. Open the doors and look at the rear one-by-twos to see if there are screw heads showing. Some cabinets will be screwed to the floor. Loosen the cabinet and fasten the weapon up under the vanity so that if it is moved, the weapon moves with it. Do not lay the weapon on the floor.

Placing a bare, unprotected weapon in this damp environment is not particularly wise. There is, however, a technique the modern hider can use to mitigate the situation. It is a vacuum-packed variation of the cache tube technology, similar to vacuum-packing meats and vegetables, and it is extremely useful for home hiders. By blister-packing your weapons in this manner you can protect them completely from the elements as long as the packages are not handled roughly or mistreated. I am using this device to protect a CAR-15 stored in the bottom of a boat under the bilge water! After more than six months, the weapon remains in excellent condition. (The example is even more remarkable because I ran the boat in salt water.)

Pistol, plastic sleeve, extra magazine, and 140-weight oil ready to be assembled into a hiding package. You may be able to obtain the four-mil. plastic sleeve required for blister packing from a butcher shop.

Few special materials are needed, and those that are, when you can find them, are relatively inexpensive. Start by purchasing ten feet of eight- or ten-inch wide, three- or four-mil. plastic sleeve. This material is not extremely common. Hiders must exercise a bit of flexibility and use whatever is available, provided it is in the ball park functionally.

Four-mil. plastic sleeves are much better than three-mil. ones because they are tougher. (Other plastic products usually will not work either. Zip-lock bags, for instance, will not seal to the extent necessary to make the system work. Also, at two mil., they are also a bit on the light side for weapons. Even the heaviest supermarket garbage bags are far too light and subject to tears and holes.) Be certain the sleeve is close to the size of the weapon. Excess width creates sloppy results.

In the past, I have used clear plastic army-surplus gun cases of Korean War vintage. New, longer, rifle sized plastic sleeves are available from butcher shops and even from stationery stores at times. Auto body and parts stores sometimes get axles or drive shafts in plastic sleeves that they will save for you. The required plastic sleeves are never easy to find, especially in the heavier four-mil. weight. Finding them is the toughest part of what is an extremely effective technique for hiding rifles and carbines. Motivated hiders simply must get on the phone and call around until they turn up a supply source.

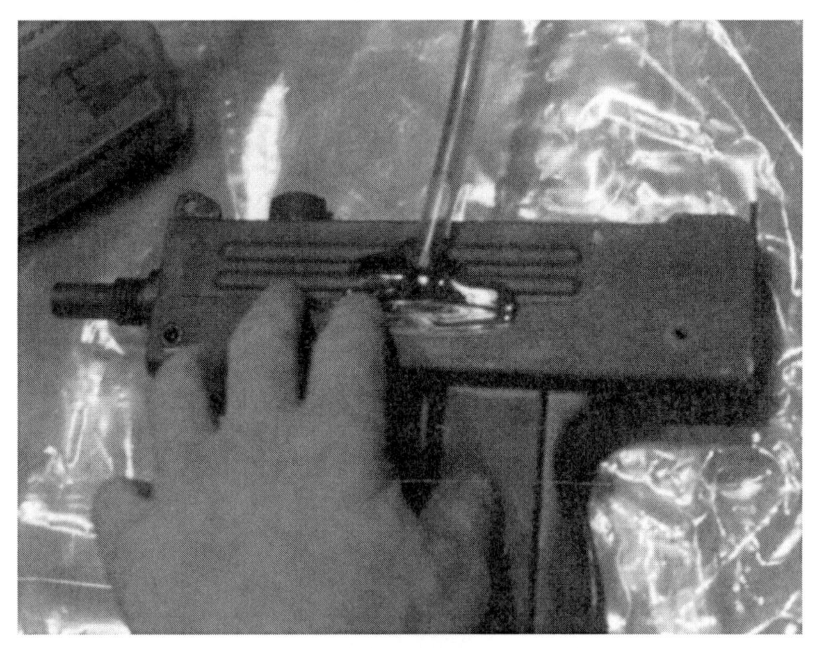

The weapon should be oiled with 140-weight gear oil before being placed in the plastic sleeve.

Once you've located four-mil. plastic sleeves, final assembly into a hiding package is decidedly easy. Coat the weapon with heavy 140 weight gear oil (available at any automotive supply store), Conoco Cotton-Picker Spindle Grease (by special order), or regular lube grease. Insert the liberally greased weapon into the plastic sleeve. Weapons such as revolvers should be loaded, auto loaders stored with a loaded clip, and military carbines inserted with a loaded magazine or two. Placing ammunition with the weapon is important if it is likely that the weapon will be removed from the hide, superficially wiped off and put immediately into service.

Weapons that are properly oiled and placed in an air-evacuated sleeve are extremely impervious to the elements. They can be stored virtually any place where the plastic will not be torn or melted.

To evacuate the air from the package, insert the weapon into the plastic sleeve and immerse in a large container of water. Be sure to keep the open "tail" of the sleeve above water.

Oiled pistol and magazine in blister pack after the air has been evacuated from the plastic sleeve. The package is now ready to be sealed.

Cut the sleeve material, which is generally sold in ten- to fifteen-foot rolls, so it is about eighteen inches longer than the weapon. (Pistols can be stored in a small pouch using the same procedure.) By leaving generous ends on the plastic sleeve, you make the completed package less subject to handling abuse that could destroy its effectiveness. This also makes the package easier to seal.

Fill a bathtub or other large container with water—a fifty-five-gallon barrel, large tank or, if one is handy, a pond or lake are ideal. Immerse the weapon and plastic sleeve on an angle so that as much water as possible covers it. (Obviously, you do not want to immerse the open end of the sleeve. Keep the extra "tail" above water.) Water pressure will force the air out of the sleeve and force the plastic to stick to the oil on the weapons. (Plastic heavier than four mil. will not shrink down and conform to the weapon as well as material of the correct weight. It is possible to use heavier plastic if one can somehow heat the water used to evacuate the air out of the package.)

Roll the sleeve end over, seal the opening with a hot iron, and tie it with a piece of nylon cord. Check to be certain the sleeve is sealed and that no air or water can leak through by submerging it in a container of water.

Sealed-up weapons can be built into false ceilings, false end walls in closets, and body panels on vehicles, where they can be kept for years. With dry wall, it is reasonably easy to place the weapon inside a wall and then replaster and paint it to look precisely as the original. Had these evacuated packets been available, French Resistance members could have placed them inside wine barrels without damage to wine or weapon.

A close friend of mine, who was forced by an unreasonable employer to work out of an office in New York City, very carefully and meticulously shortened the drawer of a file cabinet, behind which he hid a pistol. Before moving, he spent scores of hours "remodeling" his file cabinet, including calling the factory for sheet metal parts that he had a local firm shorten. When reassembled and spray painted, the shortened drawer nicely hid his Beretta pistol with two extra magazines fastened in behind. He sent the locked file cabinet to the Big Apple via commercial movers. When he arrived in town, his personal protection was there waiting for him. As a practical matter, the scheme was extremely costly since it provided only for a pistol. Perhaps the file cabinet could have been modified to accept a CAR-15, but that would have been an even more monumental undertaking.

Professional searchers often look inside the cabinets of dishwashers and TVs, but this does not completely preclude them from being reasonably good spots in which to hide a weapon. At times, an HK-94 or a CAR-15 can be placed inside the base of the cabinet where a professional might miss them. The trick in all cases is to be very careful with nails, screws, tacks, and staples so they do not look tampered with. (DEA search manuals instruct agents to tum over couches to determine whether they feel heavy and to see if the tacks and staples holding the upholstery appear to have been tampered with.)

Any of these hides will foil the casual searcher, but they will not fool the real pro. There are three additional hides available to many apartment dwellers that will work 99 percent of the time.

Assuming you can secure the help of a professional upholsterer and/or furniture dealer, it is feasible to install sleeved weapons in a waterbed. Waterbed mattresses can be professionally opened and then closed again so that the bed is usable. I have seen this hide used on two separate occasions. The owners were unclear and evasive about how they got the weapon inside the vinyl mattress. All they would say is that the factory did it for them.

If the dwelling has a basement, consider putting a regulation cache tube in the floor. The slickest scheme I have seen involved chipping through the cement to the earth below. Chipping out old concrete is a long and arduous task. It may even involve renting a small masonry hammer. This is a noisy, dirty tool that cannot be run in privacy if other tenants live in the building. If, by chance, the landlord or manager is alerted, you can claim you are putting in a radon trap.

Chipping out a round hole in the concrete by hand or with a masonry hammer involves cutting out wire or bar reinforcement placed in the concrete. This can be done with a bolt cutters or by using a cold chisel.

Remove enough concrete so that a complete cache tube will slide through the hole. Bring in a suitable post-hole auger and dig down five or six feet. With any luck, the underlying material will be clay rather than gravel. If it is gravel, it will collapse in on itself, making it very difficult to drill a clean hole. Water and bentonite clay purchased from a nursery supply store can sometimes be used to stabilize a difficult gravel bed through which a cache tube hole must be bored. After digging, insert the tube and fill the hole.

Close the hole by placing a dummy cast-iron floor drain over the opening. Use a standard floor drain purchased from a plumber. In some cases, it may be necessary to cement this fitting in place. You can also use regular window putty colored with soot to hold it in place. After a few weeks, the putty sets up hard enough to withstand traffic on the basement floor. If possible, place a rug over the drain cache and fill it up with dust from the floor. Be sure that when you are done the entire assembly looks old and untampered with.

Adventurers who have used this technique report that they worked a week of evenings putting the hide in place. Depending on your circumstances, it may be worth the effort, as this hide will almost certainly never be found. Metal detectors will be foiled by the cast-iron drain assembly and the wire in the concrete.

There is one other device worth mentioning that is so sophisticated that it might not be uncovered by professional searchers. Modern structures are usually built on two-by-ten-foot floor joists. To the hider, this means that a space about nine inches deep, fifteen inches wide, and up to three or more feet long is available between the basement ceiling and the floor above it. However, hiding in between floor joists is a fairly common device that most authorities are aware of. While it has merit, it must be done very cleverly.

Move the refrigerator out from its space in the kitchen. Carefully and meticulously lift the linoleum from the spot on the floor where the refrigerator usually stands. Lifting linoleum can be quite easy or a real bitch, depending on how well the original builders put it in and how old it is. Some older apartments will likely have two or more layers of linoleum. As a rule, the floor covering under the fridge is often in fairly good condition and can be lifted without undue trauma to it or the hider.

Once the plywood or particle board underlayment is exposed, find the exact location of the floor joists below. Various builders differ in the care with which they install floor joists. Each installation is different. Use a small nail, a ruler, or an electronic stud-locating device. Draw out a 16-inch rectangle on the floor, outlining the exact midpoint of the floor joists. This marking is critical and should be done with great precision.

Using a carbide-tipped blade on a skill saw, cut the subflooring out no deeper than the 5/8-inch plywood or 1/2-inch particle board. Doing this without cutting too deeply into the supporting joists or gouging holes in the floor takes a great deal of skill. Lift out the 16-by-18- inch (or whatever size is cut) block of subflooring. Below will be a perfect hollow spot in which to hide a weapon.

Slide the plastic weapons packet into the opening. Replace the subflooring block, puttying the cracks where the saw cut. When replaced, the piece of subflooring should rest nicely on the exposed part of the joists below. Roll back and carefully replace the linoleum. It may be wise to glue the linoleum back down lightly.

When the refrigerator is moved back over the hide, it creates an excellent psychological and physical barrier to searchers. The mass of the refrigerator along with the water pipes and electrical lines in the kitchen will tend to confuse metal detectors. Searchers might be reluctant to move a refrigerator and, if they do, they might still overlook the hide if it is constructed correctly.

These three situations are not foolproof, and they probably are not long-term solutions to what may actually call for caching. They are, however, the best there is under less-than-perfect circumstances.

The Golden Rule on hiding is fearfully simple: well trained, highly motivated officials who are reasonably certain you have a weapon hidden in your home will find it. It is possible to make their chore very difficult, and they will tear up your house or apartment in the process, but they will find a weapon that is hidden within the confines of your home. To assume otherwise is folly.

In the end, the best solution is to maintain a low profile. If the bad guys are not sure the weapon they seek is under your control, they will be reluctant to search as hard and as thoroughly as they otherwise might.

CHAPTER SEVEN

Outsmarting the Enemy

The current batch of sophisticated metal detectors available on the civilian market in the United States generally has a military background. However, it is tough to determine which carne first, the chicken or the egg. Did commercial, hobby, and police metal detectors evolve as a matter of wartime necessity, or did the Vietnam War provide the technology necessary to develop superaccurate mine detectors? We do know that most military strategists in the United States were not planning to fight a war in which a major strategical component was caching and booby-trapping. Americans have typically attempted to substitute gadgetry for philosophy, and in their attempt to deal with strategic caching and booby-trapping, they developed some extremely sophisticated devices.

As a result, cachers must contend with highly sensitive, accurate, automated mine detectors. The only real difference between the hobby devices and the standard military units is ruggedness. Military mine detectors are made to be thrown in the back of a truck—something commercial models would not tolerate for long. For a

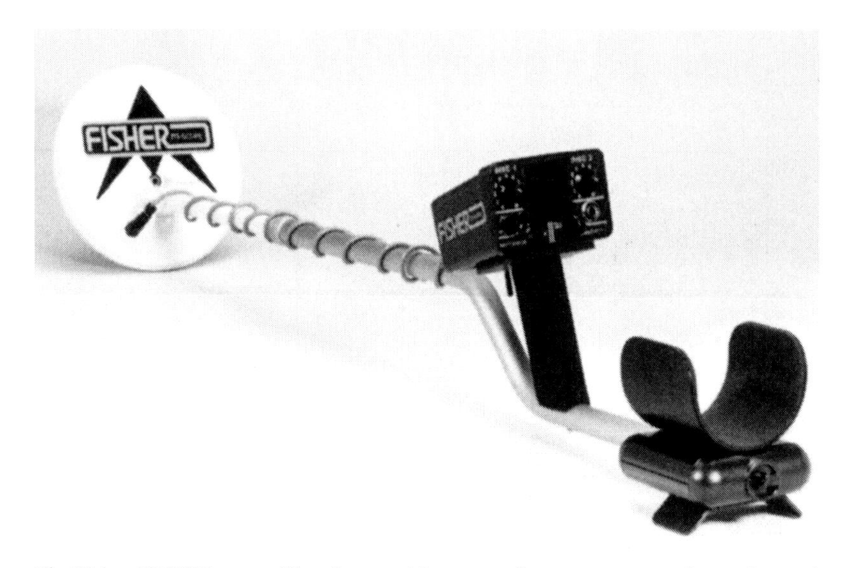

The Fisher 1265-X is a sensitive, deep-seeking, general-purpose treasure hunter's metal detector. (Photo courtesy of Fisher Research Laboratory.)

price, commercial metal detectors that will operate at up to 250 feet under water are available.

Some metal detectors exist that will consistently locate a metal pipe 35 feet below the surface or spot a penny edgewise 18 inches underground. With these gizmos, two or more people can walk 35 feet apart and thoroughly sweep a wide area very quickly.

Almost every metal detector manufacturer produces a unit that can be used under extremely difficult circumstances to find ore bodies, caches, lost weapons, pipes, and wires. They are often employed by professional treasure hunters, geologists, prospectors, public utilities personnel, and, of course, police. These sophisticated new units automatically retune themselves to compensate for wet and dry ground conditions and even for changing earth composition. Modern metal detectors can be set to scan for anything metallic, but once they pick up a buried object

Sophisticated modern metal detectors like the Compass Scanner can be used under extremely difficult circumstances and can automatically retune themselves for varying ground conditions and earth composition. (Photo courtesy of Compass Electronics.)

they can be adjusted to reject the object if it is a bottle cap, nut or bolt, or pop can tab.

Hobbyist treasure hunters do not generally use metal detectors because their weight and bulk leads to operator fatigue. Good ones are also extremely expensive, but officials looking for contraband weapons the cacher has displayed in public or has bragged about to the wrong people will not be deterred by expense or fatigue.

Conventional computerized metal detectors will find a firearms cache three feet underground 100 percent of the time. They can be set to reject most small trash, unless it has been in the ground a long time. A nail, for instance, will rust in a few years, spreading iron oxide into the surrounding ground and creating a larger target. Serious seekers won't be deterred by numerous decoys; they will simply assign some of their abundant labor force to follow behind and do the digging.

It takes about twenty to thirty hours of intense practice to become proficient with a metal detector. Because they are tiring to operate, this can be mean four or five solid days. Operators must learn how to read the signals they are receiving to determine whether their find is something of value or simply ground clutter. Very old sites that people have occupied for several hundred years or more will have a huge amount of ground clutter. Some treasure hunters claim that there are more lost coins in the ground than are currently in existence. This does not include bottle caps, nails, wire, and hundreds of similar items that are lying about.

Within the large city, state, and national enforcement groups, there are operators who spend hundreds of hours practicing, giving classes, and consulting with similar officers. Civilian treasure hunters hold regional meets where birds of a feather go to compete.

Often these people are searching for nonferrous metal, which is generally much harder to find than steel or iron. Relatively speaking, the steel used in firearms can be detected more easily and at a greater depth than anything else.

To some extent, soil conditions limit the ability of metal detectors. Historic or current tidal flats contain residual salt that acts as a deterrent. Finding a cache in salt water along the coast is a bit more difficult, but a skilled operator with the correct equipment will not be slowed perceptibly.

Some regions of the United States are characterized by extensive layers of black sand, a nickel-iron elemental material that metal detectors have problems penetrating. Much of the western United States has at least intermittent deposits of black sand that, to a small extent, will protect the integrity of a cache. Treasure hunters operating in this environment usually compensate for black sand interference by switching to sixteen-inch coils on their detector probes.

Cachers in heavily mineralized areas of northern Wisconsin and Michigan can also expect the authorities to have a tougher time finding their caches. Native iron in the soil plays havoc with metal detector readings. Still, a skilled operator who runs a metal detector over cache tubes containing as few as three rifles stored receiver down will have no trouble determining something is down there. Even where there are fairly heavy concentrations of iron, he will be able to find rifles buried a foot below the surface. The metal detector may miss one rifle, but the cacher should assume that others might be found.

In central Georgia and Alabama the soil is heavy clay with a high percentage of limonite. Again, these conditions may limit an unskilled operator to some extent, but will not deter the seasoned operator. Conversely, Georgia clay tends to have a high moisture content that will materially add to the ability of the metal detector to see down into the ground. Wet to damp conditions usually produce deeper, better readings.

With the modern, computerized metal detectors that automatically compensate for changes in ground conditions, if one moves from a black sand area to clay, the machine adjusts to a great extent. Ground conditions that fooled World War n mine detectors do not even slow down modern units. Animal excrement that confused earlier detectors, for instance, has no effect. Valid readings are made quickly and easily in pastures and corrals.

Certain conditions may sometimes baffle some operators, including old barn sites, horse pastures, and places where trash was buried, oil was spilled, welding was done, and mechanical work on vehicles was undertaken. However, unless these conditions exist in large numbers lying side by side, operator confusion is usually short-lived. If a searcher is really serious, he will simply call in members of his team to probe the entire area.

All of this makes successful caching of steel weapons sound like a losing proposition. It is true that if a skilled operator runs his coil over your cache, he will probably find it. Yet, there are several additional golden rules of caching that will assist you mightily. When judiciously applied, they will swing the pendulum back in your favor.

The first is the rule of squares. This involves the simple mathematical principle that when you double the distance from a point, there is approximately four times as much territory involved. Placing your cache not 100 feet but 200 feet out from your retreat will quadruple the territory over which the bad guys must drag their metal detectors in order to find it. At 100 feet, for example, they have 31,400 square feet to examine. At 200 feet there are 125,600 square feet involved. This is almost three acres. Take the cache out 1,000 feet or more and the search chore becomes virtually hopeless. As mentioned earlier, I believe burying in the middle of rural gravel roads is an excellent idea. Under these circumstances, your cache could range as much as five or six miles from your home.

At these longer ranges, it may pay to bury false targets, such as old bolts, nails, and trash. A search party looking as far as 1,000 feet from a retreat must thoroughly, inch by inch, cover a total of 3.14 million square feet. This is about 71 acres. Under these circumstances, 50 pounds of sixteen-penny nails scattered around would be very disconcerting.

A second rule states that the cache is less likely to be uncovered if it is located in a place that is difficult to search—where burying, mechanical work, or even stray dumping once occurred, for example. Like the Vietnamese, I would seriously consider putting a cache tube in a local cemetery if possible. Most cemeteries are open to visitors and can be accessed by car. Little rural cemeteries are much better, but some readers may not have access to these. You could almost guarantee that a cache tube in a cemetery would never be found. Ponds, streams, marshes, and lakes all fit into this category as well. A survivor in Indiana once showed me his cache tube jammed up under the bank of a creek.

A third rule involves placing the cache in a place that is virtually impossible to search. For instance, in grain bins and silos, under pig pens, and in piles of coal, gravel, firewood, or boards are all good options. These locations should be places searchers cannot check out thoroughly.

Since metal detectors do not work well in close proximity to large amounts of steel, it would be virtually impossible to locate a cache buried a foot deep in a junkyard, used car lot, or tank farm. Other than the multitude of scrap lying around just under the ground, the device would detect nothing.

Farmers and ranchers often have empty lots where they park their old, worn-out trucks, tractors, and machinery. Assuming the lot is quite large, it might be wise to put a cache tube under an old implement, knowing it will prevent the metal detector from functioning properly. This is often possible even if the lot does not belong to you.

An acquaintance in Arizona lives half a mile from an old dump that was closed in the late '50s. I suggested that he put his cache tubes in the dump ground. Metal detectors will not work at all there, and the dump site is close enough to his home that he can monitor the situation on a daily basis.

Burying in unlikely, difficult places off of your own property is almost always wise. Think seriously about placing a cache tube in the backyard of the neighborhood curmudgeon. This is the kind of person who will force the authorities to secure a warrant before they enter his property, assuming they will ever think to look there. If the location is far enough from your own property, the ruse will work every time.

It does not take much planning or bravery to creep into the curmudgeon's yard with post hole digger, tarp, and soil bags in the dark of night. Once the tube is in place and the soil carefully replaced over the hole, the cacher can return again and again in the wee hours of the morning, or whenever, to inspect and replace the weapons. Caches can be placed in an unwitting accomplice's rose bed, behind his garage, in his garden, or even inside his barn. I once stowed a plastic-sleeved .22 rifle in a neighbor's hay manger for several months, and I am sure he never suspected a thing.

Caching in difficult, unusual places where conditions are tough for searchers makes a lot of sense. Be certain, however, that the weapons that are cached predate the 1968 gun act or have been traded around informally to the point that they are not traceable by the authorities. Should Uncle Sam send his representative to the door inquiring about the Valmet assault rifle the local dealer records show as being sold to you and the weapon is hidden in your cache, you may be stumped for an acceptable answer unless you have thought that one through.

In the final analysis, the greatest single device for outwitting metal detectors is to put as much distance as possible between you and your cache. Keep a low profile when checking it, returning as seldom as possible. In some cases, it may be appropriate to visually check from the road for problems, only uncovering the actual cache every two or three years!

Conclusion

One can conclude that weapons caching, as practiced by the French Resistance and the Vietcong, will certainly be a major component of any successful late-twentieth-century military strategy. Due, no doubt, to the widespread ownership of nuclear weapons along with delivery systems that put every world leader in jeopardy, we have moved to a system of small, irregular wars. For fifty years, no country has been willing to risk a confrontation with a major nuclear power.

Warfare is not obsolete, it is just different. We now see smaller guerrilla wars where weapons caching makes more and more sense. Depending on future events, Americans may again see guerrilla warfare deployed against them. In Panama, those who happily bid General Noriega good-bye may dig up their weapons. No doubt many of those who were initially pleased with the U.S. action hedged their bets by caching a weapon or two. The vagaries of Central American politics suggest this would have been a most reasonable course of action.

Here at home in the good old US of A, state-of-the-art weapons owners in California and New Jersey are faced with the prospect of either giving up some very nice weapons or engaging in a caching program. Perhaps they do not contemplate guerrilla warfare in the short run. But these gun owners may be a careful lot who also want to hedge their bets.

Even the Communists, the fathers and mothers of the caching strategy, are faced with the prospect of weapons and munitions going underground to be used against them. Recent events indicate that capitalists who worried about the domino effect were worrying about the wrong system. It is the Communists and Socialists who are watching their systems collapse like dominos.

It might be reasonable to assume that wherever politicians control by force of arms there is also an abundance of weapons in the hands of private citizens. Gorbachev has called in all privately held rifles and shotguns in Lithuania, but one wonders how many military weapons that no one knows about are held by the Lithuanians. The second, more pressing question is how many are going underground in defiance of the government ban on weapons.

We tend to look with dismay at the situation in Lithuania, California, and New Jersey, forgetting that pistol owners in Chicago, New York, and Washington, D.C., have faced similar situations for many years now. Reputable, concerned handgun owners in these places must at least hide their weapons, even if they don't cache.

Ideally, we would all like to have our weapons on the wall, out in the open, where they can be fondled and cared for. However, this is far from an ideal world. A very few nuts often can screw it up for the rest of us.

I can easily remember the time when it was perfectly legal to own and operate military-type mortars, cannons, rifle grenades, and even howitzers. As a much younger man, I and my cohorts spent many an enjoyable Sunday afternoon firing our "monster" weapons, generally blowing things like old car bodies and bogs to hell.

Then one Saturday afternoon, three absolute nuts put on Nazi uniforms and took a Lahti 20mm antitank cannon up on a hillside outside a small New Jersey town and started punching holes through the local Democratic Party headquarters. The building was totaled before the men in white jackets got there with the required strait jackets. No one was hurt, the three clowns went to a padded cell, and the media created an atmosphere of hysteria, using the incident to the best of their ability as a rallying cry to ban all weapons of this type.

Many gun owners went along, saying, "Why not? This sort of weapon holds no attraction to me and probably has no recreational value."

As a result, some of these weapons are probably residing in caches someplace today. (Rumors to that effect surface at frequent intervals, anyway.)

Gun owners who want to go from here have the necessary tools now to cache for whatever time frame they deem appropriate. The inevitable conclusion is that we wish it wouldn't be necessary in the United States, but realistically, we know it will.